PENNY STOCKS
BEHIND THE SCENES

Beat The Promoters At Their Own
Game & Profit

DANIEL REGAN

ISBN-10: 1722962496
ISBN-13: 9781722962494

DEDICATION

This book is dedicated to my girlfriend. Without her I would have never taken the time to write down my thoughts and share my trading strategy. Thank you so much for motivating me.

Table of Contents

PREFACE

Imagine waking up, checking your email and news feeds, and finding out that today will be one of several of your monthly pay days. The difference between this paycheck and the one you receive from your full-time job is that you will receive it in one lump sum immediately after each trade. You won't have to get up at 5:00 A.M. to commute to work and spend 40 hours a week doing monotonous tasks for your ungrateful boss. Instead, you will wake up at a reasonable hour, make sure your trading system is set up correctly and will enter several key strokes through your direct access brokerage account. Most days you will spend only 45 to 90 minutes watching your computer screen and then you can call it a day, typically walking away with significant profits each time. These types of trades continue to occur month after month and anybody can profit from them! Most people that get involved in the penny stock market lose everything because they really don't understand what they are getting themselves into. They have no idea how much of an advantage the key market players involved in these markets have over everyone else. They might as well just go to a casino and put all of their hard earned money into a slot machine because the odds are better. However, this book will teach you exactly what you need to know to become a success trader.

Over the past 15 years I have amassed a great amount of knowledge regarding trading stocks and my goal is to help you to become both a profitable and self-sufficient trader. I want you to be able to understand my methodology in the shortest time period possible, but first you must realize that trading is not easy (until you understand how the market works) and the penny stock market is a very competitive arena. Stocks, in general, are inherently risky and penny stocks are at the top of the spectrum. In spite of these facts, with big risks come big rewards and if you learn how to minimize these risks, the rewards can be incredibly attractive. You will need to invest some time if you plan to be a successful trader and it will be well worth the effort.

INTRODUCTION

The penny stock markets--and in particular, the Over the Counter Bulletin Board (OTCBB) and Pink Sheet exchanges--are often referred to as the Wild West of the stock market. These two exchanges list some of the most volatile stocks in the world. Many people in the finance industry look down upon the companies and people involved in these markets. Mutual funds typically have a policy against purchasing stocks under $5.00 per share since these types of stocks are non-marginable and therefore can't be borrowed as easily. If you watch CNBC or Bloomberg, it is rare to see the people talking about penny stocks. You may have heard of penny stocks or known someone that purchased a few hundred dollars of a penny stock in their brokerage account. They may have bought them based off a newsletter recommendation, a stock tip from a friend or some other random reason. What they do not realize is the penny stock market is rigged. It is similar to going to a casino and putting money into a slot machine but instead of the 25% advantage that the casino has over you, in the penny stock market it is more like a 99% advantage. What this means is that for every dollar that you put into the penny stock market 99 cents will be automatically lost in the long-term. These are extremely poor odds and there is absolutely no reason to partake in something like this. Mark my words, if you do not know what you are doing and try to invest in penny stocks for the long term, you will lose all of your money very quickly. The reason that I know this is because I started out like everyone else that fails in the penny stock market, but luckily I learned what is actually going on behind the scenes.

In 2002 the first stock that I ever purchased was XKEM (now XKEMQ due to bankruptcy) at 10 cents per share based off a tip from a stock newsletter that promised a huge 1000% returns in the next thirty days. At the time I was young and naive and really had no idea what I was getting myself into. Before purchasing, I reviewed XKEM's profile on Yahoo Finance, checked out XKEM's website and did a Google search on the company to find out more information. I liked XKEM's pharmaceutical product Nicosan, which they claimed was being used to treat Sickle Cell Anemia disease. The company was based out of New Jersey but they stated that they had a factory in Nigeria, China, and India where they supposedly were manufacturing the drug. After reviewing all the information, it seemed the company had long-term prospects so I jumped in and purchased $1,000 of the stock. On the first day, the stock price increased to $0.12 for a 20% gain. The following day it dropped back to $0.10 and the third day it dropped 50% to $0.05! A month later the stock was trading at $0.006 and today the company is bankrupt (trading at .0001). My initial investment had lost 90%! I was certainly angry about this and wondered why this had happened, so I started searching for an answer. Unfortunately, I could not determine what had caused this stock to drop because there were only positive news released for this stock during this time period. The company also had not released an earnings report. A few months went by and I started to research more of the stocks that were profiled by this newsletter. I soon realized that most of these stocks exhibited the exact same pattern that XKEM did. I followed the white rabbit down the rabbit hole and my journey into the penny stock underworld began. From that day forward I immersed myself into the inner workings of the penny stock market in hopes of finding an answer to the question: How can a person consistently make money in penny stocks?

Please go to the following website: http://www.beatstockpromoters.com/other/files.zip to download the essential files that go with this book. The password to any files is Doji201 (case sensitive). Please download these files on a desktop or laptop computer only.

CHAPTER 1

THE PENNY STOCK MARKET
BEHIND THE SCENES

<u>What Are Penny Stock?</u>

In the world of finance, a penny stock is referred to as any stock which trades under $5.00 per share. This is not entirely accurate since some stocks listed on the NasdaqCM, AMEX or NYSE are trading under $5.00. A few of these companies are true penny stocks which have never been able to increase their share price above $5.00, yet have maintained the $1.00 minimum share price and market capitalization to stay listed on these exchanges. In general, these are very volatile stocks and many of them fit my definition of the ideal type of penny stocks that I focus on. For instance SiriusXM Radio (ticker symbol: SIRI) is a real company that trades on the NASDAQ Exchange. Its current market capitalization (price per share multiplied by the number of shares outstanding) is more than $15 billion and it earns $500 million per year in profits. This is a massive company in comparison to a true penny stock which normally has a market capitalization in between $1 million and $50 million and no earnings.

Due to its massive float, SIRI rarely moves more than $.05 to $.10 per share a day on average and, therefore, it is useless to trade.

The reality is a penny stock is not so much about the price of the stock, but rather the volatility and potential price movement that a stock can make. For instance, if I buy a $2.00 stock and the price spikes up to $20.00 I will most likely continue to watch this stock since its high level of volatility could help it continue to spike up even higher. I don't really want to limit myself to a $.01 or a $.25 true penny stock because then my profit opportunities will be reduced, and the opportunities in low priced stocks trading under $1.00 is much lower today versus several years ago.

Who Are The Major Players?

The penny stock markets have various groups of people that all play a role in the way this market functions. Many of these groups will be explained more thoroughly in later chapters, but I want to give short introductions. The first group and one of the most important are market makers. These are no longer human beings (like they were in the past) but rather computer algorithms which are designed to "make a market" in a stock, and ultimately take advantage of the uninformed, unsuspecting retail investors and traders. They typically have complete control over what happens in all of the securities, and it is important to learn how they operate.

Another important group is institutions. This includes hedge funds that deal with small and microcap stocks. Not only does this group trade in some of these lower price stocks for their clients, but they are also involved in providing funding usually in the form of dilutive financing for numerous penny stock companies.

The most important group of people in the penny stock market is the stock promoters. These people decide when and for how long a penny stock is going to rise. Insiders such as upper management of publicly traded companies are also tied into these stock promotion groups because they usually decide when they are willing to pay for a stock promotion in order to help increase the price of their company's stock. Another group is large retail traders because these wealthy and successful traders play a major role in this market. The main reason for this is because they decide whether they are willing to commit large sums of capital in order to provide liquidity and support the price of these types of stocks. Smaller retail traders are another group which is involved in this market although they don't play a huge role because the capital that they commit isn't enough to affect the price of penny stocks. Finally, the uninformed individual penny stock investors are a large part of this market because they are preyed upon by all of the other groups. These people provide most, if not all, of the capital that pays the salaries of all of the other major players in the penny stock market.

Stocks That I Focus On:

In general, the penny stocks that most people seem to be interested in trade on the OTCBB and Pink Sheet exchanges (which is now called the OTCQX exchange) and have either (.OB) or (.PK) extensions added to their 4 digit stock ticker symbol. Unfortunately these stocks are not as liquid as they used to be. Listed stocks such as lower-priced NASDAQ CM, NYSE or AMEX stock are also volatile and can make large percentage moves in a short period of time just like OTC penny stocks. In recently times the OTC market has been a lot slower than it was prior to the end of 2013, but these small and microcap listed penny stocks have been heating up and creating tremendous opportunities.

The OTCQX exchange has approximately 12,000 companies listed on it most of which can be considered amongst the worst managed companies in the world. For the most part, almost all of these companies refer to themselves as being in an "exploratory stage." What this means is that they are start-up companies with perhaps a great idea for a product or service but little if any financing to produce or market their product or service. Most of the time they lack the management and employees needed to operate a company successfully. A majority of these companies have a price per share somewhere in between $.0001 and $10.00 per share but I mainly focus on penny stocks in between $.10 and $20.00.

If a stock starts out at $1.00 and runs up above $20.00+ per share in a short period of time (which does happen), I still consider this to be a penny stock. There are some stocks listed on these exchanges with a price per share of anywhere from $10.00 to $150.00 but I completely overlook these companies since most of these companies are actually legitimate businesses that earn a profit but choose to stay listed on the OTC because the regulatory requirements are much lower, and therefore less costly, than on the bigger exchanges. For instance to be listed on the OTCBB Exchange, a company must file certain documents with the SEC like an annual report called a 10K filing, but there is no set date of when they must release their earnings like a typically listed stock. On the Pink Sheets, companies are not required to file earnings reports unless they choose to. This market is, therefore, a free-for-all and the companies can more or less do whatever they want. Uninformed penny stock investors that buy into these stocks thinking they are a great long-term investment almost always learn the hard way!

I know this will sound crazy especially because this guide is based upon how I occasionally buy these companies, but the truth is that stocks listed on these exchanges are nothing more than trading vehicles. What this means is that money will flow in and out of these penny stocks and the majority of the money flow never actually remains for more than a few minutes to several days. You have to get comfortable with this simple fact or you will never be able to handle the psychological side of trading penny stocks. It really does not matter what a company says they do, whether they manufacture a product or earn a profit (since almost none of them do). They are merely created to trade in and out of in hopes of earning a short-term profit. If you can grasp this concept now, it will be much easier when you actually begin to trade. If you are somebody that gets attached to your investments and really wants to believe in a company's story, the penny stock market is not for you.

<u>What Are Big Board Stocks?</u>

A big board stock is the name given to a stock of a company which is publicly traded on the NASDAQ, AMEX, or NYSE exchanges. When somebody refers to "The Market," also known as the Dow Jones Industrials (DIA), S&P 500 (SPY), NASDAQ (QQQ), or the Russell 2000 (RUT), they are referring to these types of stocks. These are the exchanges which list the stocks of the largest and most successful (and many less successful) publicly traded companies in the world such as Google (GOOG), Apple (AAPL), or General Electric (GE). While it is possible to make thousands or even millions of dollars trading these stocks there are a few reasons that most people are turned off by them.

Fortunately despite the name of this book, my trading system does allow me to trade higher priced stocks when high probability opportunities arise, and I certainly do trade them on a daily basis.

First, in order to buy 100 shares of GOOG stock which currently trades around $890 per share, you have to put up $89,000. Such a small amount of shares of a stock with this high of a price tag really is not very much. For instance, if GOOG's average daily range is $10.00 per share (approximately 1.1%), you have to capture the entire daily range, which is very difficult when day trading, just to make $1000 profit. A $1.00 stock with an average daily range of $.15 (15%) and $55,000 position, would earn you a whopping $8,250! Reducing your position to a more manageable $15,000 in this same penny stock would result in a more than double profit in one day if timed correctly. I don't know about you but I would rather put $15,000 at risk rather than $67,000. Nonetheless if you have enough capital to trade higher priced stocks, there are many opportunities to profit day in and day out and everyone reading this should have a goal to trade any priced stock eventually.

Another reason trading higher price stocks is more difficult is because the stock market is full of some of the most intelligent people in the world, and they are all focused on big board stocks. While I consider myself to be of above-average intelligence, I do not believe I can compete with rocket scientists turned quantitative analysts, financial engineers and other individuals who are involved in sophisticated trading strategies like high-frequency trading. Many of these people work for large institutions which supply them with hundreds of millions or even billions of dollars in trading capital. It is just not possible for the average person to compete against these people in the short-term trading of well-known companies on a consistent basis, but it is possible to extract profits if you know what you are doing. Long-term over many years, if you buy the right stocks in the right industry, you most likely will make money but it is very difficult to beat the average market returns because you have to deal with recessions which result in 20-60% draw down (declines in the overall market)! Fortunately the less followed and higher priced stocks do not follow the market as much, so I focus more on them.

Although the penny stock market is certainly rigged and therefore heavily manipulated by the key market players, fortunately in the penny stock market you go up against degenerate gamblers and uninformed penny stock "investors." I found the website in the figure below while searching Google for the term "penny stock." The only thing that this person is doing right is using money that they **can** afford to lose. I can think of a lot of better ways to waste $500 because 99.9% of the time a person like this will lose all their money very quickly. See the figure below.

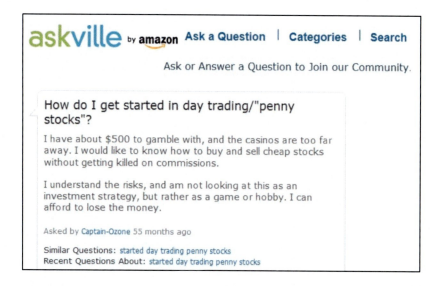

I refer to these types of people as "Kool-Aid drinkers" because they are completely oblivious to what the penny stock market really is (although this person seems to admit they are a gambler). They could be a desperate person that buys a penny stock hoping it will go up 10,000% so that they can quit their miserable job or an 80-year-old retired guy that buys a penny stock based on a paper newsletter that he received in the mail touting the next AAPL stock. They could also be somebody that buys a penny stock based off of a tip from one of their golf buddies whom told them it was a sure thing. Since these people think of the penny stock market like a casino and have no idea what they are doing, they are most definitely consistent losers. Therefore, if you know the correct patterns and how to identify the correct stocks at the right time, you will be able to take their money! Essentially this is the purpose of this guide and in general, this is the whole purpose of trading: How to take somebody else's money (legally) who is less informed than you.

Correct Time of Day to Trade

The stock market is open for normal business during regular trading from 9:30 A.M. to 4:00 P.M. Eastern Standard Time. Premarket electronic trading begins at 4:00 AM, however it does not usually become liquid enough to trade until 8:00 A.M. The premarket trading ends at 9:30 A.M. After-hours electronic trading begins at 4:00 P.M. and ends at 8:00 PM. In general, even though the stock market is open for 16 hours each day, there are only specific times when trading can be potentially profitable. Basically, these times are 9:30-11:00 A.M. EST and 2:30-4:00 P.M EST. Given the proper catalyst (earnings releases, deal news, etc.) pre-market trading from 8:00-9:30 A.M. EST and after hours trading from 4:00 to 5:00 P.M. is okay as well. It's very important to understand that the rest of the time there is a good chance that you will lose money if you trade. The reason for this is because as a trader you need volatility in the form of stock price movement, in order to earn a profit. Near the open at 9:30 A.M. the volatility is very high and stocks usually make their biggest price movements. The market maker's computer algorithms have little control over stocks when the volatility is very high. Near the close in between 3:15 and 4:00 P.M., stocks sometimes make decent size moves because large institutions usually place their buy and sell orders at this time. In the middle of the day stocks usually do absolutely nothing or pull back hard to shake out all the suckers who don't realize that this time period is not for trading. If you trade from 11:30 A.M. to 1:30 P.M. there is a high probability that you will lose all your money since you will go up against the market making algorithms and it's extremely difficult to beat a computer consistently.

The only time you should consider trading a stock in the "dead zone" from 11:00 to 2:30 is if a stock has a specific catalyst such as a news release or a strong technical setup. This is also true of premarket and after-hours trading. When you trade during the premarket or after hours, all trades are electronic. This means buy and sell orders are matched automatically and the market makers are not trading for their own account in between the bid/ask spread. For this reason, the volatility is usually very low but the spreads are very wide, which means stocks can make fast moves. If you are on the wrong side of the market during this time, you can lose a lot of money very quickly because stocks trade very "thin." For this reason, you need to make sure that you have a significant catalyst such as earnings or some other news release which causes the volume to rise to a level which is way above its 20-day average. Without this sort of catalyst, you will be trading against the computer algorithms and you just can't win at that game.

Penny Stock Scams:

Most of the penny stocks that I trade are outright scams or really crappy start-up companies in their early stages. I also trade real companies especially when trading bounce plays in strongly oversold stocks or short sales in overextended stocks. In recent times there have been many of these non-OTC stock trading opportunities. Even though I actually like trading penny stock scams, as a trader we must adapt, so that is what I have done as the number of OTC penny stock trading opportunities has declined. When I say scam, I really do mean a total fraud. I am not kidding! For the average person it is very hard to comprehend buying crappy companies (even though most penny stock investors do it constantly without realizing it) but buying an outright scam would be completely incomprehensible for most people. I am sure you are thinking why would you want to put your hard earned money into a scam? Please read on and I will elaborate.

In order for a company to continue as a going concern, i.e. stay in business, it must generate cash flow. In order to generate cash flow, it must have a marketable product or service which generates revenue for the company. Before a company can produce this product or market their service, they need to obtain financing. The purpose of going public in the first place is to raise funds but the funds generated from an initial public offering IPO (an initial public offering is when a privately owned company takes their company, splits it up into shares of stock and then sells itself to the public) are only received once at the time of the IPO and they can quickly run out if a company isn't generating any profits. Once these funds are depleted an unprofitable company must find another way to get additional funding or they will have to file for Chapter 11 and go bankrupt. Since most penny stock companies do not generate any revenues or profits they will have a hard time going to the bank for a commercial loan. They also will not be able to cover interest payments required from issuing bonds, i.e. debt, so this type of financing is usually out of the question as well.

The only three alternatives that remain are to commit accounting fraud-- completely make up profits, cover up losses and hope that nobody finds out (See Enron and World Com). In the process, they can probably obtain financing which is occasionally what some penny stock companies do (Google search: Spongtech - SPNG scam to find out about this). Alternatively, a company may attempt to increase the price per share of their company's stock by generating investor awareness and then perform what is called a secondary offering. A secondary offering is when a currently public company issues more shares to the public. What this essentially does is provide them with more funding to stay in business but in the process dilutes the value of the current shareholders' stock, which causes the price of the stock to fall. This occurs because the shares outstanding increase and therefore the price per share of the stock will decrease.

The last alternative is normally the way that most penny stock companies stay in business and it usually comes in the form of an SEC filing called form S8. Companies can occasionally obtain funding from a private equity firm or a hedge fund by issuing shares of their stock to these firms at a steep discount (usually 50 - 90%) to the current market price of the stock. This type of funding is commonly referred to as "death spiral" funding which is very dangerous to share holders and one of the main reasons why penny stock "investing" is so risky. Most of the time when a penny stock spikes a large amount in a short period of time this type of dilution will occur within 1-3 days.

Penny Stock Promoters: Pure Evil
or Angels In Disguise?

Here is where we get into the good stuff! A stock promoter is a person or business entity that is paid to bring investor awareness to a stock. This is typically referred to as a "pump and dump." Essentially the only way for these crappy or fraudulent companies to attract investors to their stock and generate enough buying volume to purchase the shares that they issue is to do an S8. An S8 is essentially a form of dilution to current shareholders which is also known as a secondary offering. They do this in order to cover payroll and pay for other expenses (such as taking a private jet to the Maldives for a long weekend) since they have no earnings and cannot take out a bank loan.

See the figure below of the chart of a classic pump and dump. Notice the stock goes up for a few months from $.80 to $6.50 per share without any major pullbacks. This is called "The Pump Stage." Eventually, the stock has a catastrophic day where it completely collapses losing all of its gains in a matter of a few minutes. This is called "The Dump Stage." In this case, the stock dropped from $6.50 all the way down to $.90 in a very short period of time. The dump stage is always much shorter than the pump stage.

This consistent increase in the price of the stock is due to an incredibly successful stock promotion and the subsequent dump is due to a third party shareholder selling millions of shares of the stock to unsuspecting penny investors that believe the company is real. Many stock promoters can only dream to manipulate a stock this well. This stock promotion that took place in JAMN stock occurred in between March and June 2011. The stock promoter involved in this promotion was Hackthestockmarket.com, which is also known as Doublingstocks.com and Daytradingrobot.com. The compensation was approximately $2.5 million. Hackthestockmarket.com no longer is taking new subscribers and they haven't put out a new promotion in several years. Their websites are down as well.

What these companies do is set up an offshore entity that cannot be traced back to them. Sometimes a large majority shareholder with deep pockets may also pay a stock promoter to try to help increase the price of a company's shares for their own personal gain. Both of these individuals are referred to as a "third party." The cost of a stock promotion campaign ranges from a thousand dollars up to several million dollars. The amount of money that a stock promoter can charge is dependent upon their reputation which is based on their track record of assisting clients with increasing the price of their worthless penny stock scams. A stock promoter that can bring $10 million of buying volume into a penny stock in one day or $50 - $300 million of volume over a month is at the top of the ladder and will be compensated the most.

A stock promoter that brings one hundred thousand dollars into a stock for one day will be compensated much less and may only be able to cause a short-term increase in the price of a stock for a few minutes. In either case, the buying volume that these stock promoters generate is temporary and completely artificial. Sometimes the purpose of the stock promotion is to increase the price of a stock but other times it is just to increase the buying volume regardless if the stock goes up or not. Ultimately only the promoter's client knows what they want to occur in the stock but we can try to figure out their plan by watching the volume and price action. If the buying volume is high (relative to the 30-day average volume) but the stock is not moving up, there is a good chance that a third party is just dumping stock at the current price. If the volume is high and the stock is rising, the third party may be selling a little bit of stock but not enough to overpower the demand for the stock. This type of price action should lead to higher prices.

Anytime you see a penny stock listed on the OTCBB or Pink Sheets that has increased by 20% to 10,000% or more in a short period of time (a few minutes to 12 weeks at most usually), there is a very good chance that a stock promoter is involved. Paid stock promotions are now also occurring in NASDAQ, AMEX or NYSE stocks as well. For example, occasionally a stock promoter will take a large position in a stock and then send out emails to their subscribers. The reason that they do this is in order to increase the price of a stock in order to sell the shares that they own to their unsuspecting subscribers. A perfect example of this occurred in the stock BroadVision Inc. - (BVSN), which increased from $8.00 per share all the way up $56.00 in two months. This was a successful stock promotion by Jonathan Lebed, National Inflation Association (NIA) and Wall Street Grand. An entity named NIA (owned by Jonathan Lebed) owned approximately 200,000 shares of BVSN stock in the $8.00 range and sold at least part of their position for a several million dollar profit. They were able to do this thanks to sending out thousands of emails to their email subscribers along with overconfident short sellers, which caused a tremendous spike in this low float stock. It is also alleged that they had a hedge fund working with them to help prop up the stock and trap short sellers. Stock promotions seem like they should be illegal, but as long as promoters disclose their position, surprisingly they are not.

Press Releases:

News stories that are released online or in print tend to have a positive or negative effect on stocks. The reason for this is that as new information becomes available to the market, market participants, or the computer algorithms that they utilize, buy or sell a stock, based off of this new information. I am not just referring to earnings, because these type of releases certainly effect stocks, but also contracts with big successful companies, potential mergers or acquisitions, FDA approval, patents, government contracts, or some other types of positive or negative market moving news. There are online news services which will give you access to real-time news for a fee of about $20-50 a month although certain brokers may also provide this for free. Here are a few of these services: Fly On The Wall, Business Wire, Global Newswire, and PR Newswire. While these can be useful for intraday trading non-OTC stocks, the news stories that I follow are usually released while the market is closed and, therefore, you can get them for free from a website such as Yahoo Finance. Nonetheless if you plan to day trade, having access to real-time news is a necessity and $20-50 a month is a minuscule amount to pay when you can earn thousands of dollars by utilizing these types of services.

You probably will not believe me when I tell you this but the type of penny stock scams I am referring to release fictitious press releases. Most of the time unscrupulous companies will release these news stories at the beginning of a stock promotion campaign and sometimes they even release a series of consecutive press releases during each day of a stock promotion. One way a company will bring a lot of attention to their stock is to get the name and ticker symbol of a successful stock in the same industry, in one of their own press releases. Most news stories that you read on penny stock companies are issued through a service like PR newswire which only cost $200 and is syndicated to many ultra-high traffic websites online like Yahoo Finance. They may seem legitimate but they are not! For instance if a penny stock company claims to be in the consumer electronics industry and their main product is a futuristic cell phone battery that only needs to be charged once every 6 months, they may state that they have entered into an exclusive partnership agreement with Apple (AAPL) to supply their battery to be used in the production of the next Apple iPhone release.

This type of news will usually cause a 100-300% gain in a penny stock in a short period of time. I am not certain how they are able to get away with this (especially now that the SEC started an penny stock task force) and honestly, I do not really think they do over the long-term, but in the short-term this type of news will cause a significant increase in the price of a penny stock. Most of the time the penny stock company will release a follow-up press release stating that the agreement has been terminated or the partner company will release a statement saying they have no idea who the company is and why they are claiming to have a partnership. Either way, the important part for us as traders is that the ticker symbol will show up on other traders' news scanners and the increase in volume from the article will show up on traders' volume scanners, which will bring significant attention to the stock. In recent years penny stock companies which claimed to have deals with social media sites like Facebook, have also had the same sort of violent spikes in the prices of their stocks.

Another type of news release that is very common when dealing with these blatant scams is when a company does what is called a "Reverse Merger." A merger is when a legitimate company essentially agrees (or is forced in the case of a hostile takeover) to merge together with another company. Legitimate mergers almost always cause a large increase in a stocks volume and this can result in a stock price to rise. A reverse merger is a shady tactic that penny stock scammers use where a private company is taken public by merging into a shell company. A shell company is a public company that has been registered in a certain industry such as gold mining but has no operations of any kind and is usually nothing more than a registered business entity.

Many times when a penny stock scam is uncovered by the market after a pump and dump has occurred, a company will change its name and ticker symbol and reverse merge into one of these shell companies. For instance, a so-called exploratory oil and gas exploration company called ABC exploration may reverse merge into a shell called XYZ Healthcare. Ask yourself this: Why on earth would an oil and gas exploration company miraculously change their business model to focus on the health care industry overnight? I have been asking myself the same question since 2002 and the only answer that I have come up with is that these penny stock CEOs are the greatest con artists of our generation! Either that or penny stock investors are the biggest fools alive (definitely true). Almost everyone of these stocks that does a reverse merger will get a lot of attention from degenerate gamblers and penny stock investors, so companies usually release news that coincide with the beginning of a stock promotion campaign and a reverse merger. Essentially reverse mergers look like IPOs but they are not. These are just a few examples of bogus press releases but I can assure you that 99.9% of the news that you read on most high volume penny stocks is made up. I mean it! Needless to say, these type of blatant lies actually help us to make money so I am all for them!

Methods Used by Stock Promoters:

In order for stock promoters to help to inflate the price of a company's stock, they have some common tools that they can use. The first and one of the oldest ways is through the use of scummy stock brokers that cold call individuals. If you have ever seen the movie *Boiler Room* or more recently *The Wolf Of Wall Street,* you will know what I am referring to. These companies target geographic locations such as Boynton and Delray Beach, FL where the population is mainly wealthy retirees, as well as areas in the Western U.S (Idaho, Iowa, etc.) where the population may be older and less educated (i.e. farmers and blue collar workers), but not necessarily poor. This method is less common today because it requires hiring employees and renting office space which is more expensive than new modern methods that are currently being utilized. None the less, there was recently a promotion on a stock where brokers were used to pump up the share price, so cold calling is still being used today. The employees of these companies are paid a commission which is referred to as a RIP, which is a percentage of the stock that they sell to unsuspecting victims. The stocks that they suggest to these random strangers are the same stocks that companies pay stock promoters to promote. The SEC cracked down on this sort of thing around 2002 after the Dot Com Bubble burst. Since a lot of worthless penny stocks were trading in the $10.00 to $80.00 range rather than in the $0.01-$10.00 range where they are now, it was easier to convince suckers that these were real companies.

Yet another type of stock promotion involves sending out paper newsletters which I usually refer to as mailers or pump mailers. These are normally sent in a regular sized envelope through the U.S. Postal Service or occasionally in a larger envelope through UPS or Fedex. They are normally sent from stock promoters opt-in address book where you have to provide your name and address to receive them. Occasionally I believe some legitimate companies also sell our personal information because from time to time I have received mailers which I have not signed up for. Mailers usually have 1-20 pages of worthless information and completely exaggerated claims about a penny stock such as stating that a stock is expected to rise 10,000% in the next month. These type of mailers are sometimes very effective if the stock promoter has a large enough subscriber base. The number of mailers that go out to suckers is dependent upon the size of the budget that a stock promoter is allocated by the third party to pay for printing supplies and postage. Promoters with thousands of addresses and a strong track record will be the most in demand. In 2014 there are many fewer mailer promotions than there used to be a few years ago and they are typically lasting less time than in the past (1-2 weeks instead of a month).

See the figure below for the first 2 pages of a mailer which promoted the stock of Horiyoshi Worldwide Inc - (HHWW) in December of 2010. Notice how the company compares themselves to a real company True Religion - (TRGL) which was also in the same industry. True Religion is a legitimate high-end clothing retailer which is still in business today. In 2004, they convinced consumers that it was acceptable to spend $300 on a pair of jeans and started a new trend for high-end designer rip-off clothing. HHWW tried to mimic this companies success by claiming their stock price would spike up similar to TRGL's stock which experienced a massive spike in their stock price. HHWW claimed they were selling tee shirts for $120 each and had deals with high-end clothing retailers like Saks Fifth Avenue and online retailers like Amazon. The only problem was that Saks Fifth Avenue did not sell this company's products and when I contacted a Saks Fifth Avenue employee regarding HHWW, they had no idea what Horiyoshi Worldwide was. When this stock eventually collapsed I actually wrote an article on my Facebook group devoted to trading detailing how I had traded this stock and I actually had one of the stock promoters contact me claiming that the company had contacted the SEC and were investigating a "smear" campaign that had brought down the stock from $3.50 to $1.00 in a few minutes. They also told me that they thought I was somehow part of the group that had caused the stock to collapse which is quite comical. What they forgot to mention was that a third party had sold hundreds of millions of shares of this stock essentially causing it to collapse. In the process, they profited millions of dollars at the expense of uninformed penny stock investors that believed they were going to become millionaires. The funny thing is that lucky early investors in HHWW stock actually had gains of 400% but the suckers that hold these scams for more than a few days to a week ALWAYS lose all their money.

Like *True Religion* Before It, Shares In This Company Could Explode By 4,538% Before Summer of 2011!

The biggest names in movies and music are already wearing high-end *Horiyoshi the III* clothing, and just like shares in jean company *True Religion* shot from $.67 to $31.08, shares in Horiyoshi Worldwide (HHWW) could soar even higher before Summer, 2011!

A jump that big means $5,000 turns into $226,900 - $10,000 grows to $453,800

Fellow Investor,

At an estimated $600 Billion, it's no secret that the fashion industry is big business...

But did you know that a healthy chunk of that $600 Billion, roughly $41 Billion, is in the niche of "designer" fashion?

Now, if a company were to garner *just half of a percent* of that niche market, they'd be looking at $205 Million in revenues.

However, the world of fashion is as cutthroat as any other business and making a name for yourself is next to impossible in this dog-eat-dog industry.

Horiyoshi the III display at Saks 5th Ave

With fashion you need an edge, an ace in the hole – something to get your foot in the proverbial door...

And nothing builds your brand better than your products being seen on Hollywood's elite, which is something that Horiyoshi Worldwide is already doing.

Big A-list celebrities like Johnny Depp, Angelina Jolie and Brad Pitt to some of the biggest names in music like Gwen Stefani, Mick Jagger and The Black-Eyed Peas have all been seen wearing the exclusive apparel of Horiyoshi the III...

As raved about in...

VOGUE

The New York Times

Style

Inked

International Herald Tribune

2011, it may be too late.

And that "cool" factor is quickly turning into public demand. High-end retailers like Nieman Marcus, Fred Segal and Harvey Nichols are gobbling up as much Horiyoshi as they possibly can.

But it's Horiyoshi Worldwide's upcoming street-wear collection that has investors chomping at the bit, because once this more affordable line hits the stores, profits will go through the roof.

We've seen this buying rush happen before with denim designers *True Religion*, whose shares exploded from $.65 to $24 in less than a year...

And now's the time to lock in your profits by investing early in HHWW, because by Summer

As seen in...

Saks Fifth Avenue

HARVEY NICHOLS

Browns

Maxfield

Ron Herman

Horiyoshi: Proving Lighting (and Profits) Can Strike Twice

There's a reason why experts are predicting big things for Horiyoshi Worldwide – and it all starts with *True Religion*...

Another method that is currently used is called opt-in fax marketing. This type of stock promotion basically consists of sending out faxes with information about a penny stock that is identical to the information sent out in paper mailers. Not that many people are using normal fax machines anymore so this method isn't very common. None the less, it is called opt-in marketing because I believe by law it is illegal to send an unsolicited fax like this but I know I have received some of these without giving my consent, so I assume these stock promoters break the law. I am not even sure if that many people even use fax machines anymore since scanning a document and attaching the file to an email is so easy.

The most common form of stock promotion today is called opt-in email marketing which I refer to as "pump emails". It is "opt-in" because there are thousands of free penny stock alert websites that send out emails touting hot stocks that they "claim" will experience a large price increase in a short period of time. In order to get emails from these websites, you have to go to each website and input your email address (and sometimes your name --use a fake). Most of these websites charge you nothing for this service. Can you guess why? Right, because they are being paid by penny stock companies to promote their stocks and they need suckers to buy them. There are also premium pay sites that send out the same type of email alerts and these are just as bad as the free sites except the premium sites have convinced suckers to pay them for their crappy penny stock alerts. I do not suggest to ever paying for a stock picking service like this.

Occasionally you may also see actual spam emails promoting a stock. While these used to be a lot more common, they are not as prevalent anymore because the United States passed laws to reduce the amount of spam emails being sent. Despite this fact, I occasionally still receive unsolicited spam emails with stock recommendations, however, these usually just end up in my spam box now. None the less, spam emails can sometimes cause penny stocks to spike.

Another method that is used today is SMS text messages or even instant message alerts. These two methods are less common but are starting to show up on the websites of certain stock promoters. The premise behind these alerts is the same. The promoter says on their website that these type of stock alerts are faster than email alerts and, therefore, you are getting an advantage over other subscribers of their newsletter or stock picking service. Once they have your email and phone, they can bombard you with as many stock touts as they want so I suggest buying a disposable phone for $20.00 if you would like to sign up for these type of alerts.

The final method that is relatively new but is most likely to become more common is video marketing. Some promoters have started to send a DVD through the mail or post You-Tube videos online, promoting their next big stock pick. The rationalization as to why these videos work is because people believe that it must cost a lot to create a DVD and, therefore, the stock promoter must know what they are talking about or else why would they spend their time and money? This is obviously wrong but I hope suckers continue believing this load of crap so I can keep taking their money!

It is All In The Stock Promoter's Disclaimer:

Out of all of the methods I have just listed, there are only three important things to focus on. The rest of the information provided by a stock promoter is useless. The first is the ticker symbols of the stocks that they promote. You will want to make note of any tickers that you see through pump emails, faxes, pump mailers, DVDs, websites, and phone calls related to penny stocks. The second is the date that you first receive notice of a stock promotion or if you are lucky, an upcoming promotion. The third and single most important piece of information is **"The Disclaimer"**, which is always at the bottom of the email, fax, paper mailer or at the end of the DVD, in very small fine print. See the figure below for an example of a disclaimer. You'll want to read this disclaimer thoroughly. You can skip the entire part of the advertisement besides these three pieces of information above but definitely keep track of the date you receive any of the above. The reason for this is by law a stock promoter has to disclose a few key pieces of information in their disclaimers. The first thing is how much they have been **compensated**. Sometimes this is in numerical form: $500,000 and other times in word form: Five Hundred Thousand Dollars (if the promoter is smarter since very few people bother to read the fine print and older people with poor vision may not even be capable of reading it). This amount is very important to keep track of because the larger the compensation, the more successful a stock promoter's track record has been and, therefore, the higher the probability that their stock pick will increase by a large amount. I normally use Crtl+F to do a keyword search for dollars or $ so I don't have to read the whole disclaimer. The only problem with this is sometimes promoters attach their disclaimer as a jpg file, and therefore, you won't be able to do a key word search. I believe promoters can overstate this amount but I am certain they cannot legally understate it. From my experience, any compensation above $500,000 usually means a stock promotion will run for more than one day although this is definitely not a guarantee, especially if the stock gaps up 100% or more right when the alert is released.

The second piece of information that they must disclose is whether they, their friends, family or a third party, own a position in the stock that they are promoting. The reason for this is that occasionally really crappy penny stock companies that cannot even raise $10,000 to pay a stock promoter will instead pay the stock promoter with shares of their companies stock. The reason a stock promoter may accept this offer is because if they can bring enough buying volume into a stock to significantly increase the price of the stock, then they can sell their shares at a higher price and most likely earn a large profit. Also, sometimes a large investor will accumulate a large amount of a company's stock but will then have nobody to sell to. If they buy 10 million shares of a penny stock trading at $0.50, they cannot exactly put in an order to sell 10 million shares all at once. In order to sell-off a position this large it may take several months due to the illiquidity of penny stocks which may only trade 50,000 shares a day on average. However, if they pay a stock promoter $500,000 to help bring $10 millions of buying volume into the stock over a five day period then they can most likely liquidate their position at for instance $1.00 per share. This would yield a profit of $4.5 million after taking into account the fee paid to the promoter. This sounds like a great deal and I believe this is very common in the penny stock market.

The last piece of information to be aware of is that many times promoters will state the length of their stock promotion contract to be for instance two days or one month. They do this to try to convince penny stock investors that the promotion will not end abruptly and that the promoter is committed to the success of the profiled stock. I do not believe there are any laws against misrepresenting this information and, therefore, you should not rely on it. Also from my experience promoters usually completely lie about this information. For this reason, I suggest referring to historical data and instead assume that the current stock promotion will last the same amount of time as their last one. Refer to the historical chart of the stock and see how many days the stock spiked up the last time they released a promotion (usually anytime you see a high volume spike in the historic hart of and OTCBB or Pink Sheet stock, a promotion has taken place). This may not always be the case but as I mentioned above, promoters get compensated based on their past performance and it is rare that a stock promotions lasts for more than a few days.

I know all of this seems downright illegal but as far as I know it is not illegal as long as the promoter discloses the proper information in their disclaimer. Knowing how the whole process works helps me to profit from their shady business practices and, therefore, I am thankful that stock promoters continue to do this. See the figure below of a disclaimer for a stock promotion on the stock HHWW from the same newsletter above. Also, notice how hard it is to read.

IMPORTANT NOTICE AND DISCLAIMER: This featured company sponsored advertising issue of Breakaway Stocks does not purport to provide an analysis of any company's financial position, operations or prospects and this is not to be construed as a recommendation by Breakaway Stocks or an offer or solicitation to buy or sell any security. Horiyoshi Worldwide, (HHWW), the company featured in this issue, appears as paid advertising, paid by Lux Media Corporation to provide public awareness for HHWW. Lux Media Corporation has approved and signed off as "approved for public dissemination" all statements made herein regarding Horiyoshi Worldwide's history, assets, technologies, current as well as prospective business operations and industry information. Breakaway Stocks and Capital Financial Media (CFM) have used outside research and writers using public information to create the advertisement coming from Breakaway Stocks about HHWW. Although the information contained in this advertisement is believed to be reliable, Breakaway Stocks and CFM makes no warranties as to the accuracy of any of the content herein and accepts no liability for how readers may choose to utilize the content. Readers should perform their own due-diligence, including consulting with a licensed, qualified investment professional or analyst. Further, readers are strongly urged to independently verify all statements made in this advertisement and perform extensive due diligence on this or any other advertised company. Breakaway Stocks is not offering securities for sale. An offer to buy or sell can be made only with accompanying disclosure documents and only in the states and provinces for which they are approved. Many states have established rules requiring the approval of a security by a state security administrator. Check with http://www.nasaa.org or call your state security administrator to determine whether a particular security is licensed for sale in your state. Many companies have information filed with state securities regulators and many will supply investors with additional information on request. CFM has received and managed a total production budget of $3,600,000 for this advertising effort and will retain any amounts over and above the cost of production, copywriting services, mailing and other distribution expenses, as a fee for its services. Breakaway Stocks is paid $3,000 as an editorial fee from CFM and also expects to receive new subscriber revenue as a result of this advertising effort. *More information can be received from Horiyoshi Worldwide's investor relations firm, or at Horiyoshi Worldwide's website http://horiyoshi-thethird.com. Further, specific financial information, filings and disclosures as well as general investor information about publicly traded companies like Horiyoshi Worldwide, advice to investors and other investor resources are available at the Securities and Exchange Commission website www.sec.gov and www.nasd.com. Any investment should be made only after consulting with a qualified investment advisor and after reviewing the publicly available financial statements of and other information about the company and verifying that the investment is appropriate and suitable. Investing in securities is highly speculative and carries a great deal of risk especially as to new companies with limited operations and no history of earnings. The information contained herein contains forward-looking information within the meaning of section 27a of the Securities Act of 1993, as amended, and section 21e of the Securities Exchange Act of 1934, as amended, including statements regarding expected growth of the advertised company. In accordance with the safe harbor provisions of the Private Securities Litigation Reform Act, Horiyoshi Worldwide notes that statements contained herein that look forward in time, which include everything other than historical information, involve risks and uncertainties that may affect the Company's actual results of operations. Factors that could cause actual results to differ include the size and growth of the market, the Company's ability to fund its capital requirements in the near term and in the long term; pricing pressures, technology issues etc.

Why does the SEC Not Crack Down on these Scams?

Honestly, I have been asking myself this question for eight years and I have never been able to come up with a definitive answer until recently when the SEC started a new task force who's main objective is to shut down these penny stock scams. In the past, I had two guesses why these scams continue to exist. The first was that the SEC had way too much going on to deal with penny stock scams. The reason I thought this was because there are at least 12,000 OTCBB and Pink Sheet listed stocks in existence. Considering I believe that the majority of these companies are downright scams, the SEC did not have nearly enough resources to monitor or investigate all of these companies, but their new task force might help to change this. In the past, the only reason they seemed to get involved in shutting down a scam was after a successful long-term pump and dump occurred and one of these stocks dropped 50%-70% in one day (this is very common). Under these circumstances, there were many suckers that had lost everything that they invested in a penny stock. Occasionally are some degenerate penny stock investors that take out home equity loans for several hundred thousand dollars and lose it all in a matter of minutes when a stock plummets. In the past some of these people sometimes file a class action lawsuit against the company and several months after the pump and dump is finished, the company will be investigated and halted by the SEC. This used to be very rare, but in recent months, the SEC has been shutting down some alleged pump and dump scams in as little as one week. What this means is the time horizon for these promotions has been cut down a lot and now it's not a good idea to hold these for more than a very short period unless you are holding them on the short side and betting against the stock.

The second answer that I had to this question is that our government really liked to collect tax revenues from these penny stock companies and, therefore, would rather have left them alone until they caused major issues that could not be overlooked. For instance, when a stock went from $0.20 to $2.50 in one month (rising by potentially hundreds of millions of dollars in market value) due to stock promotion and then dropped back to $0.80 in one day and $0.10 one month later, this brought unwanted attention to a penny stock. This sort of rise in price added hundreds of millions of dollars to the market cap of penny stocks in a short period of time and when it disappeared in 20 minutes, the authorities had to take a closer look and ask questions. Since they finally created an eight-person task force to police these scams, I am not sure if this is true anymore.

CHAPTER 2

MODERN TECHNICAL ANALYSIS

<u>What is Technical Analysis?</u>

B y definition technical analysis is the art of evaluating stocks and other securities by analyzing statistics generated by market activity, such as past prices and volume[1]. It is a way to explore the inner workings of the market and what is really going on behind the scene in terms of the market participants and the psychology which drives securities prices. Technical analysts do not attempt to measure a security's intrinsic value like a fundamental analyst but instead use stock charts and other tools to identify price patterns that may suggest the future direction of a stock. Most technical analysis focuses on the short or <u>intermediate-term</u> and is based on three <u>major</u> beliefs:

(1.) **History repeats itself:** The reason that technical analysts believe this is due to the fact that the stock market is made of a group of buyers and sellers that are all analyzing the same pieces of information. For the most part, human beings are very predictable and although computer algorithms are playing a much bigger role in the stock market, they too are can be predictable as well. Financial professionals must say past performance is not indicative of future performance in their disclaimers but in my experience, this simply is not true.

(2.) **Prices move in trends and usually follow known patterns:** A trend in the stock market is defined as a period of higher lows and higher highs. In general Isaac Newton's Law of Motion which basically states an object in motion tends to stay in motion, unless an external force stops it, applies to stocks. In the case of a heavily promoted penny stock scam (which is extremely manipulated) a trend is usually defined as a period of higher highs with no higher lows. Essentially the stock goes straight up with no major pullbacks. Patterns form in the stock market due to the fact that people trade off of technical analysis which is a self-fulfilling prophecy. Since everyone is looking at the same chart and perhaps the same indicators, they sometimes come to the same conclusion, which causes patterns to form and people to buy or sell a stock. Fear and greed also play a large role in the formation of specific price patterns.

(3) **The current market price of a stock includes all available information:** The reason for this is that technical analysts believe that all available information is factored into the price of a stock. Even when information is material and non-public, certain people will acquire this information and trade off of it illegally. By monitoring price and volume on a company's stock chart, a person is able to find clues which would not otherwise be visible to fundamental analysts.

How did I learn Technical Analysis?

The way that I learned technical analysis was by reading many books and then applying what I read to various stocks that I had been watching at the time. This takes time and won't happen overnight. Even though many technical indicators are basically useless and some of the information in older books is outdated, certain principles of technical analysis remain valid. I took hundreds of trading ideas and indicators and applied them to my trading until I found a group of technical indicators that actually complemented each other. In the process, I filtered out hundreds of indicators and methods that are completely useless which is basically what all of the unprofitable traders focus on. I will cover these principles in the next section however I would highly advise you to purchase a book such as <u>Technical Analysis of Stock Trends, 9th Edition by Robert D. Edwards and Jon Magee</u> to get a better understanding of the fundamentals of technical analysis but just understand that the information in a book like this is just to build a foundation, not to make trading decisions.

<u>Why Do I Utilize Technical Analysis?</u>

Considering the fact that almost no penny stock companies earn a profit and very few if any even have the prospect of earning one, it would seem foolish to think that one could actually analyze fundamental data such as P/E ratios and earnings growth, to determine the intrinsic value of one of these stocks. As I said earlier, penny stocks are nothing more than trading vehicles because they have almost no chance of ever earning a profit. DO NOT LISTEN TO ANYONE THAT TELLS YOU THAT YOU CAN DO FUNDAMENTAL ANALYSIS ON PENNY STOCKS! I refer to them as ticker symbols and could not careless about what the company claims that they sell or the services they provide because it is all pure lies. Stocks of real companies are valued on future expected earnings but penny stock companies will never earn a profit, so they cannot be valued the same way. Despite this fact, there are thousands and thousands of people that believe XYZ penny stock will someday earn $1 billion a year because a stock promoter's newsletter said that the stock is trading in a $30 billion industry. The reason for this statement is that $1 billion is only 3.3% of the entire market share in the industry, but what the promoter forget to mention is that XYZ is nothing more than a shell company in a specific industry with a flashy website and a great idea for a product, but absolutely no prospects of ever becoming a profitable company. For these reasons technical analysis works very well when applied to penny stocks because you are trading based off of patterns which are formed by the fear and greed of uninformed market participants. Analysis of price, volume, and their derivatives, are the only factors that you should focus on when trading.

Useful Technical Indicators:

There are hundreds of technical indicators and for the most part, they all do the same thing. Whether it be Stochastic, MACD, Money Flow, OBV, CCI or Accumulation/Distribution, all of these have two things in common. First, many of them tell you exactly the same information so it does not matter if you use one or one hundred of them. Secondly, all indicators are lagging because they are calculated using historic data and, for this reason, they show you what has occurred in the past. They do not forecast what will happen to the stock price in the future and, therefore, have little if any predictive value. On top of this, most people try to use the standard default settings on all of these indicators. Thirty years ago you could make a lot of money following the basic rules of buying when the stochastic indicator with default settings, was below 20 and selling when it got above 80. Unfortunately due to high-frequency traders and other computer algorithms, most of these technical indicators are now useless and the market has become much more competitive and efficient. What this means is that somebody now takes the opposite side of your trade, because the statistics show that these indicators, with default settings, no longer work. Professional traders know that the general public will continue to use them essentially throwing away their money away and putting it into the pockets of the smart money (informed traders and market makers.) I am not saying they have no value at all. However, you have to configure the indicators differently than the default settings and choose the right indicators. For these reasons I avoid most of these indicators and instead I focus group of specific ones.

I occasionally look at an RSI on daily chart with a setting of 13 days, rather than the standard setting of 14. I use 13 because this is a Fibonacci number and I find using these numbers work better. The RSI indicator is a momentum indicator which shows overbought and oversold conditions in a stock. It ranges from 1 to 100 with a reading below 30 being oversold and due for a potential reversal, and a reading over 70 being overbought and due for a pullback. I also added a Bollinger Band to the RSI so that I can see when the RSI indicator is breaking out of the bands and when the bands are contracting. The settings I use for the Bollinger Bands are 1.25 Standard Deviations and a period of 50. I use a combination of these two indicators to determine where a stock is in terms of its trading range and project what should happen if the RSI breaks out. I do not use the indicator to generate signals to buy or sell like the technical analysis books say you should but I find that when a stock approaches a reading below 8 or above 93, there is a higher probability of a reversal of some sort in the near future. It could occur in as short as a minute or as long as several day or weeks, and, therefore, this indicator should be only be used for confirmation. Note that stocks can stay overbought or oversold for longer than you would expect due to early short sellers being squeezed higher and early dip buyers losing all their money, as the stock drops a lot more. I also focus on and RSI reading of 50, 61.8 or 76.4 because these are Fibonacci levels and I find that these are potential reversal points.

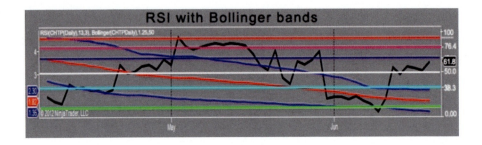

Support and Resistance:

This is the single most important factor for a technical analyst in my opinion. Support is the price level at which demand is thought to be strong enough to prevent the price of a stock from declining further. The logic dictates that as the price declines towards support and gets cheaper, buyers become more inclined to buy and sellers become less inclined to sell. By the time the price reaches the support level it is believed that demand (buyers) for a stock will overcome supply (sellers) and prevent the price from falling below the support level. Resistance is the price level at which selling is thought to be strong enough to prevent the price from rising further. The logic dictates that as the price advances towards resistance sellers become more inclined to sell and buyers become less inclined to buy. By the time the price reaches the resistance level, it is believed that supply will overcome demand and prevent the price from rising above resistance.

To simplify, if a group of people bought a stock at $1.00 and it immediately dropped to $.50, when it eventually trades back to $1.00, a majority of the previous buyers will want to sell the stock for breakeven (this is basic human nature). This selling pressure will create a resistance level which will prevent a stock from rising any higher. The opposite is the case for a support level. If a group of people buy a stock at $1.00 and it immediately rises to $1.50, they may be inclined to buy more of the stock if the price drops back down to $1.00. This creates a support level because buyers support the stock and prevent the price from going lower.

To draw a support or resistance level, you need a stock to bounce off a specific price level two or more times. Once this occurs you can draw a straight line through these two points and this will show you the important levels where buyers or sellers may affect the direction of a stock. The more times a stock hits a support or resistance level, the stronger the move will be when the stock finally breaches this price level. In lower priced stocks a support or resistance level will usually fall within a few cents of a previous price level where the stock put previously reversed. In a higher priced stock ($10.00 or more) this level may be a larger range of $0.15 or even $1.00 or more away from the previous level. See the figure below for a basic example. I could probably write a whole book on support and resistance but there is more than enough information already written on this subject. I highly suggest that you read more and familiarize yourself with this concept. Understanding support and resistance is one of the most important parts of learning to become a consistently profitable trader because it is the basis for risk management which will be explained later in this guide. Please understand that this is price based support and resistance, but there are many other types of resistance which I refer to as hidden resistance later in the book.

Japanese Candlestick Charts:

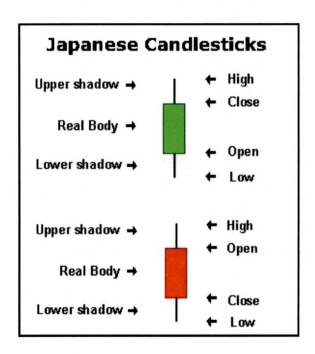

The best way to determine support and resistance is to pull up a chart of a stock. I personally use Japanese candlesticks in my charting because I feel they help display a clearer picture of what is actually going on with the price action of a stock. There is always a constant battle between buyers and sellers, i.e. the bulls and the bears and the candlestick charts will give you a view into which group is winning the battle. Japanese candlesticks are calculated by taking the open, high, low and close of a stock and drawing them on a chart (see figure below). Many candlestick patterns are constantly recurring in the market. I cannot list all of them, but a few of my favorite patterns are hammers (bottom reversal), Doji's (indecision: potential continuation or reversal), Bearish or bullish engulfing (reversal), Bearish or bullish Harami (reversal), Tri-tips (reversal), Tweezer bottom or tops (reversal) and shooting stars (topping reversal). I suggest searching online for these terms and also familiarizing yourself with other candlestick patterns. It will take a little while to get comfortable spotting these patterns but you will soon realize how important they are in trading. On a day in which a stock finished positive, a candlestick will typically be colored white or green and the stock's closing price will be above its open. If the stock's close was lower than its high, then the candlestick will have an upper wick. Also, if the stock's low was below the open, the stock would have a lower wick. If the stocks close was below the opening price, then a candlestick will typically be colored red or black.

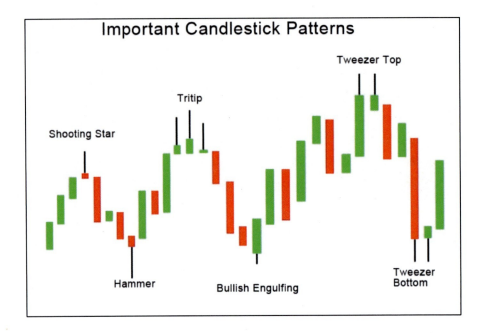

Important Candlestick Patterns

Start out with a daily chart (each candle is one day of price data) and look back at 3, 6, 9 and 12 months (sometimes more) of historic price data. Try to locate price levels on the chart where the stock peaked at least two or more times. The more times that a stock touches a specific price level and fails to go higher (resistance) or lower (support), the more important these support and resistance levels are. Now use a ray or horizontal line drawing tool in your charting program (I personally use Medved Trader for charting stocks but there are a few others that will work such as Esignal (expensive) to draw a straight line through these points. To get a copy of the software go to Medvedtrader.com and download it from there. The software is free to use with just one chart by utilizing the built in end of day stock quotes provided by yahoo finance. Alternatively to get real time stocks quotes (which is a necessity for day trading) you'll need a real time data source (more on this later). Since you will need more than one chart you will need to purchase a monthly subscription. The cost is about $20 a month which is extremely reasonable considering some trading software costs as much as $1,000 a month for basically the same thing. A lot of new traders try to trade using free software and the problem with this is that the cost of trading software is a barrier to entry which keeps uninformed people from becoming successful. Therefore it is in your best interest to pay for this software so that you can take advantage of them.

Once you have the software make sure that the trend lines extend to the right essentially projecting a line into the future. As I said before, these points do not have to be at the exact same price but a range of about plus or minus $0.01 to $0.15 is usually fine depending on the price of the stock. With higher priced stocks you need to give a little bit more room for price noise around a support or resistance level. Repeat this process until you find all of the points in the last year. Once you do this, you will also need to to identify support levels where the stock was dropping and did not continue to go any lower. In general buying, a stock in between support and resistance levels is not a good idea. It is best to buy a stock near a support level after a stock has tried and failed to break through the support level at least twice, but preferably three times. It is best to sell near a resistance level or sell into the increased buying volume that occurs due to a breakout above a resistance level on the third attempt.

Notice in the figure below how former resistance levels become new support levels once a stock breaks through them to the upside. Also, notice how former support levels become new resistance once a stock breaks through them to the downside. This is a very important concept to understand since it is the basis for the way that all stocks move. Note that once a stock first breaks through it generally will pull back towards the support or resistance level to "test" the buyers or sellers and find out if they are strong enough to hold the stock above new price level. This happens 99% of the time. The same thing occurs on a breakdown below support. A stock will almost always bounce back up and test the price level to see if the sellers (shorts) are still in control.

Fibonacci Retracements:

Leonardo Fibonacci was a mathematician in the 1600's that realized that there was a sequence of numbers in which a number added to the number preceding it would equal the next number in the sequence. Below is the beginning of the sequence.

1, 1, 2, 3, 5, 8, 13, 21, 34, 55, 89, 144, 233, 377, 610, 987, 1597

When you take one of these numbers and divide it by the number that precedes it, you come up with a series of ratios. For some reason, these ratios are very prevalent in the movement of securities such as stocks. The most common ratios are 23.6%, 38.2%, 50%, 61.8%, and 76.4%. The way that you can incorporate these ratios into your trading is by taking the swing high and swing low of a stock and drawing the Fibonacci retracement levels. After a stock makes a move up or down, it will typically pullback to one of these Fibonacci ratios before the stock will find support and move higher. For instance, if a stock moves from $.50 to $1.50, it typically will retrace 50% of its the range to $1.00 before potentially moving back up to attempt to breakout above the previous high at $1.50. These retracements happen about 98% of the time.

When you draw a Fibonacci retracement, you need to take a swing low to a swing high when interested in buying a stock, and a swing high to a swing low when interested in shorting a stock. This is not set in stone because if the buyers in a stock are very strong the stock could instead pullback just 23.6% of its range to $1.35 before continuing higher. It could also pullback to one of the other ratios such as 38.3% at $1.19. If the stock is weaker, it could even retrace to 76.4% of the amount it moved up to $1.12. You do not know which ratio will be important for a specific stock so you want to watch all of them, but **61.8%** is called the golden. This ratio is the main turning point where congestion (pullbacks) or trend reversals in a stock will take place most of the time assuming a stock spiked up to this level quickly. For instance, if a stock rises from $1.00 to $2.00 it almost always will pullback and find support around $1.38, before moving higher. 50% is not a Fibonacci ratio but it is the second most common area where stocks will find support or resistance and reverse. I do not know why these ratios work so well but I can guarantee you will be amazed when you start to draw these retracement points on your charts and realize you can pinpoint where a stock will pullback to. Just be aware that due to the fact that many people know about these important price levels, most of the time these Fibonacci level will be tested two or more times to determine if they are valid. Do not be surprised if you buy a stock on a pullback to a 61.8% retracement price level and the stock immediately spikes $0.15 per share and then swiftly comes back down to test the same 61.8% price level a second or third time, to try to shake buyers out.

These Fibonacci retracements will work in stocks, options, futures, commodities, currencies, etc., on all time frames from tick charts, to 1 minute, to daily, weekly and monthly charts. I suggest you do a Google search on Fibonacci ratios for trading and familiarize yourself with these ratios and figure out how to use the Fibonacci tool in your charting software to draw these retracements. Combining Fibonacci retracements with other areas of technical analysis is one of the keys to profiting in the stock market. See the figure below and notice how the stock pulls back to the 23.6 Fibonacci price levels. After a stock moves up a large amount it will usually pullback more than this, so you can expect a move lower to the 50% or 61.8% levels at $0.7609 or $0.7454, (which are shown in orange) before the stock has a chance to move higher.

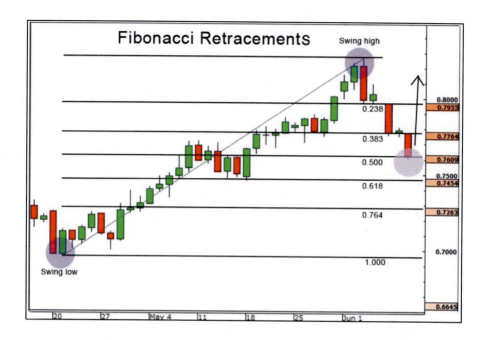

A unique tool which you will not find in any books I call the Fibonacci buffer zones. Stocks rarely if ever reverse the first time they hit the Fibonacci retracement level. While the stocks will usually spike up or drop very quickly due to traders placing their limit orders at these retracement levels, the stock almost always comes back down at least one more time. This occurs either to bounce off the same price level and tests buyers or moves a bit lower to what I call the Fibonacci Buffer Zones. The zones I use are 23.6% to 27.1%, 38.3% to 41.1%, 50.0% to 54.5%,, 61.8% to 65.6%, and, 76.4% to 78.6%. For instance, in the figure below the stock first pulls back to the 23.6% Fibonacci level before bouncing momentarily and then quickly comes back down and bounces at the 27.1% level. Sometimes the stock will reverse here and move back to the previous high, but most of the time it will continue lower until it eventually reaches the 61.8% to 65.6% buffer zone. Occasionally if the stock is weaker or the prior up move was very large, a stock will go even lower to the 76.4% and 78.6% zone. This happens in larger priced stocks a lot more than lower priced penny stocks, but occasionally this occurs on over extended pump and dumps. If a stock does not reverse at or near the 78.6% retracement level, then you can usually assume that the trend has reversed and should expect a large move to the downside.

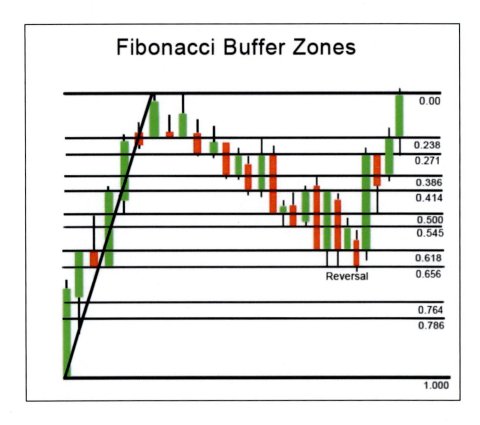

Fibonacci Extensions

Whereas Fibonacci retracements help to project potentially turning points during pulls backs, Fibonacci extensions help to project turning points after a stock breaks out above a resistance level when going long or breaks down below a support level when going short. Therefore, they can be used to "project" which price a stock should move towards and at which price it should pullback or completely reverse. Fibonacci extensions are the basis for all price movement in the world's financial markets because they can be constantly calculated as new price action occurs. They work in all asset classes and on all time frames from second charts to minute, daily, weekly and monthly charts. Fibonacci extensions are the holy grail of technical analysis. Successful traders know this and guard this secret with their lives while unprofitable traders continue to search for an indicator or trading system that never loses. I know this because I have seen many trading alert services which base their buys and sells off these price levels, but never explain to their subscribers how they are arriving at these targets. They do this because they realize if their subscribers find out, they will no longer subscribe to the alert services and then these guru's will have to go get a real job rather than fleecing there subscribers out of their money. Although Fibonacci extensions will not work every single time, in my experience they work at least 75% of the time. You won't know which Fibonacci level the stock will reverse at, but specific levels usually act as strong hidden support and resistance levels. For this reason it is imperative that you understand that everything in trading is based on probabilities and nothing will work 100% of the time. For this reason you must place stop losses just under one of these levels and in the event that an important Fibonacci level is breached, you exit the stock immediately. When you are aware of these levels, you can set targets and offsetting stop-loss orders which result in a sufficient risk/reward profile.

The most important Fibonacci extension levels are 123.6%-127.1%, 1.386%-1.414%, 161.8-165.6%, 261.8%-265.6%, 361.8%-365.6% and 423.6%-427.1% because trend reversals typically occur at these price levels. At the 123.6%-127.1%, 138.6%-141.4%, 150.0%-154.5% and Fibonacci extension levels, prices usually just pullback but the trend remains intact. Notice once again I have used "buffer zones" since prices don't always move to an exact price level and reverse. Normally, the lower the price of the stock, the better the chance that the stock will come very close to reversing at the exact Fibonacci extension levels. They will typically hit the 161.8% first and quickly pullback and then spike higher hitting the 165.6% Fibonacci extension level, before ultimately pulling back a significant amount and breaking the previous important support level. The reason these quick price movements occur is because market participants usually place their limit orders around these levels causing a sharp pullback or spike in the price. Market makers and smart traders also program their algorithms around these levels as well which adds even more fuel to the fire. Very few people realize that the long wicks on certain Japanese candlesticks are formed when prices hit these important Fibonacci extension levels. The two most notable examples of this are hammer and shooting star candlestick patterns.

In order to draw a Fibonacci extension on your chart, you need three points. Some charting software will have a Fibonacci extension tool built-in whereas other software will only have a Fibonacci retracement tool. If your software only has a retracement tool, refer to the figure below for a better understanding of how to draw Fibonacci extensions. Start out at a swing high - point A and drag your Fibonacci retracement tool down to the swing low - point B. Next, click on the line at the 0.000 retracement level which should pass through the swing low at point A and drag this line up so that it passes through the swing high at point C (red line). You should now notice that the Fibonacci retracement levels will now be above the current price level. These levels will now act as resistance. You may need to add these Fibonacci extension levels by going into the options menu or right clicking the actual Fibonacci retracement in your charting software since the levels that I use are not standard and, therefore, are not widely known. The extension levels have a 1 before them because they are essentially calculated by taking a specific price range and multiplying it by 1.0 + (a Fibonacci extension level). For instance, 1.0 + .618 will give you 1.618 or the 161.8% level, the next Fibonacci extension. Once you understand how to draw theses Fibonacci extensions, you can find the next extension level as soon as you have a new swing high, swing low and the price reaches the previous swing high/low. Fibonacci extensions can also be calculated for short sale trades by starting point A at a swing low up to point B at a swing high and back down to point C at the previous swing low. Everything else is the same except this time the Fibonacci extension levels will act as support levels where short sales should be covered or bounce trades may occur.

When combined with the other trading tools such as Fibonacci retracements, Fibonacci time cycles, etc., you will have a very strong understanding of where price is headed in the future. Fibonacci extensions are incredibly effective in trading and I suggest doing more research to learn more about this important trading tool.

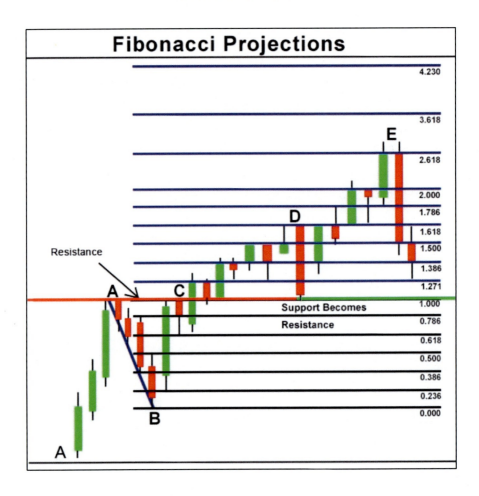

Fibonacci Time Cycles

Fibonacci time cycles are a tool which can be used to project areas where a stock may pullback or completely reverse in the future. By combining these time cycles with other indicators such as Fibonacci retracements, Fibonacci extensions, support and resistance and pivot points, you can become fairly accurate at forecasting key turning points in any type of security. The two most important Fibonacci levels are 138.3% and 161.8%. Notice in the figure below how an initial cycle is drawn from point A (swing high) to point B (swing high) using the

Fibonacci time cycle tool. The number of candlesticks in this cycle is 42 (you can also draw the cycle using a swing low to a swing high.) Lines are then projected into the future by calculating 38.3% and 61.8% of the previous 42 candlestick range. This results in a line being plotted at the **16** = (42 *.383) and **26** = (42*.618) candlestick marks. Notice how the turning points were projected within one candlestick. As is the case in the figure below at point C (38.3% level), you usually see a sizable pullback, however, the trend typically remains intact and the stock moves higher. At point D (61.8% level) complete reversals in the trend typically occur. In the example below I used this tool on an intraday chart however, it works well on daily, monthly or weekly charts as well. I suggest reading more about this indicator because it is very powerful for forecasting important reversal points. Please note if your charting software does not have a time cycle or Fibonacci time zone tool then you can just manually do the calculation by counting the candles and plot a line to use as a guide.

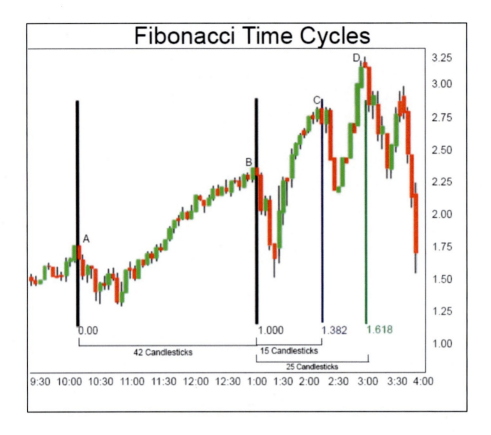

Symmetry: Measured Move

For some reason, stock movement tends to be symmetrical. This occurs for both price and time and is usually referred to as a "measure move". Refer to the figure below for a better understanding of the symmetry of price movement. Notice how the stock moved up from point A at $1.00, to point B. at $1.50 and then pulled back to point C. at $1.25. Next it continued to move up again breaking the swing high resistance level at point B and then continued to move up another $.50 from the bottom of the pullback at point B, to the target at point D. at $1.75. I refer to this as a 1/2 measured move. After the stock gets to the 1.70 area, it will usually pullback about 50% to 61.8% of its previous range and either reverse or pullback and then continue forming the next measured move.

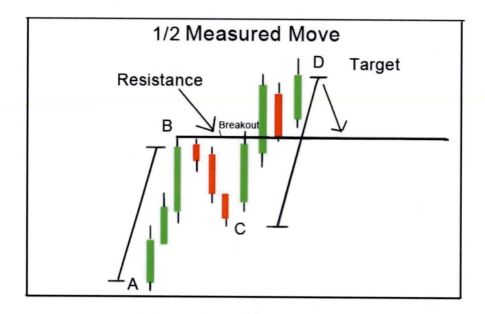

In the second figure below which I refer to as a full measured move, the distance from point A to point B can be used to project the target at point D, by adding the distance from point A to point B, to the breakout point at the resistance level. Notice how the stock retraces to the 61.8% Fibonacci retracement level before moving back up and breaking out. This type of price movement continuously occurs in the financial markets. As I mentioned earlier, the 50% and 61.8% are the most common retracement levels. Also, notice how the stock pulls back to the breakout point once resistance is broken and then spikes straight up to the measured move target at point D. These type of moves usually occur very quickly and you are either on the correct side of the market or you will be stopped out. If you look for this type of price movement, you will almost always have an idea of what to expect next. Having an idea and then reacting to the true outcome, can make you a lot of money in the market. Note that after a measured move occurs stocks usually pullback sharply, before consolidating and the next measured move begins. Measured moves are very powerful and I suggest you read more on the subject of the symmetry of stock price movements.

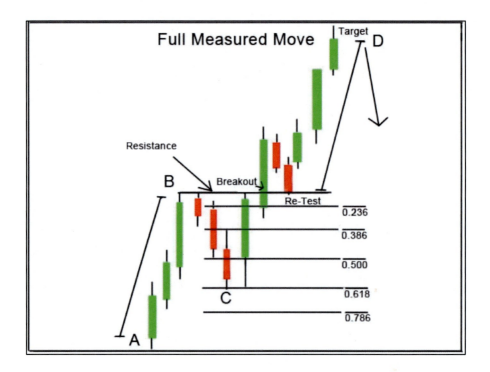

Elliot Wave Theory

While I am not a firm believer in strict adherence to the Elliot Wave Theory, there is no question in my mind that stocks move in specific, defined waves of price movement. I do not suggest trying to count waves inside of waves inside of wave, but it is a good idea to at least be familiar with the Elliot Wave Theory so you can have a better understanding of the framework for the way stocks move. When you get comfortable with how stocks move you will have a better understanding of what a stock "should" do under most circumstances.

Knowing what "should occur" a certain percentage of the time will allow you to size your positions correctly and execute solid money management strategies which are essential to profitable trading. This will allow you to be more confident in your trading decisions and stick to your plan. You never can be certain about what a stock will do, but as a trader, you have to look for patterns that form where the probability of the stock doing what you expect, is in your favor. Elliot Wave formations are one of these patterns.

The general Elliot Wave Theory says that stocks move up or down in a five wave sequence and pullbacks occur in a three wave sequence. While this is not always the case due to variations in the sequence, for example, five ways up move and four-wave down move, more often than not it occurs in all asset classes and in all time frames. For this reason, every wave can be broken down into another wave sequence, which can be broken down into yet another wave sequence, etc. Waves 1, 3 and 5 follow the trend and waves 4 and 5 are countertrend pullback waves. Waves A and C are corrective waves and wave B is a counter-trend pullback wave. Wave 3 is the longest wave in the uptrend and should not retrace more than 76.4% of the Wave 3 up move. Pullback waves 2, 4 and B usually retrace 38.3 to 76.4% of the waves that precede them, with 61.8% being the most common retracement. Corrective waves almost always occur two or more times as fast as the up or downtrend that preceded them on higher volume. When Wave C is completed, for the stock to remain in an uptrend and continue to push higher and form wave 1, the stock should not drop below the beginning of the wave 1 up move. Once you understand that all securities move based off of these wave formations, you will have a better grasp of what to expect in the future. These wave sequences do not form 100% of the time but they form more often than not. See the figure below.

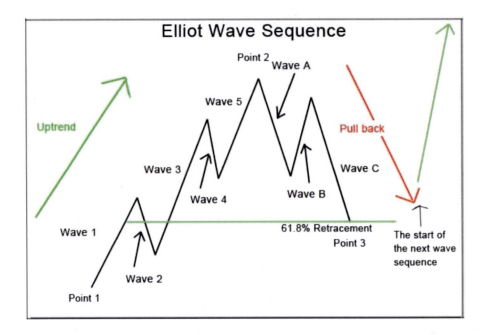

Elliot Wave Sequence

Point 2
Wave A

Wave 5

Uptrend

Pull back

Wave 3

Wave C

Wave 4

Wave B

Wave 1

61.8% Retracement
Point 3

The start of
the next wave
sequence

Wave 2

Point 1

Trend Lines & Parallel Channels:

Another form of very useful support and resistance is the parallel trend channel. Parallel channels make up the framework for the way all securities move. Many people try to draw these channels asymmetrically, however, I find a parallel channel works the best and most people do not know about this simple yet powerful trading tool. In order to draw a channel, you need three points. Point 1 is a swing low, point 2 a swing high and point 3 is a swing low. When drawing an uptrending parallel channel connect point 1 and point 2 with a straight line (called a trend line) and make sure the line extends into the future (right side of the chart). Now copy this line and place it so that the beginning starts at point 2. Trend lines are very useful in stocks for support and resistance, just remember a stock can break above or below a trend line and the trend can still remain intact as long as the candlestick does not close below that line for more than one candlesticks. Also, pay attention to the volume when a trend line is penetrated because a low volume penetration is usually short lived. Parallel channels should give you an idea of where the price of a stock is headed and where it may find support and resistance in the future. You can draw both up channels and down channels the same way, just reverse the order of the points. When price breaks out of a channel, it usually will eventually form another area for you to draw a new parallel channel. Sometimes security will breakout of the channel and then fall back inside resulting in a failed breakout. When a stock fails to traverse the channel and touch the opposite trend line, there is a good chance the trend may be changing and it could be a good sign to exit a stock. In general, it is good to buy near point 3 and sell when the stock gets to the upper channel. You can also wait for a breakout through the upper trend line and if the stock fails, sell your position. See figure below for a visual representation.

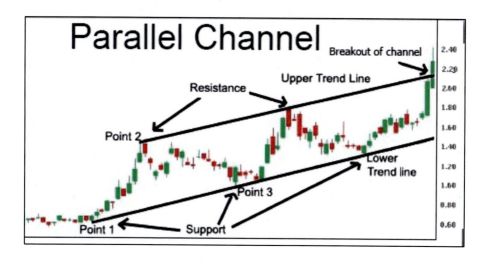

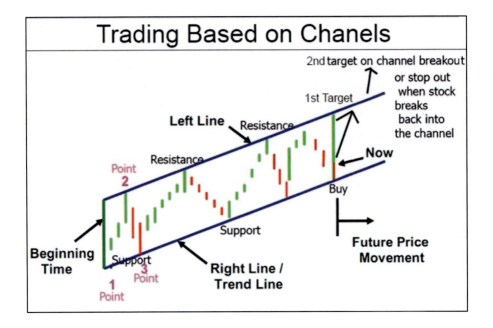

Once you understand how to find the three points and draw a trend channel, it is possible to project continuous channels. What this does for you is give you an idea of the short, mid and long-term trend, as well as helps to forecast where the stock will most likely head in the near future. I define turning points in a stock as FTT's or "failure to traverse" the channel. All securities move back and forth across these parallel channels. I do not know why they move this way but they always have and will probably continue to move like this. The Fibonacci retracement levels that I discussed earlier in this chapter play a large role in how far a stock pulls back before continuing higher inside of these channels. They also help to understand the framework for the way stocks move. When a stock does not traverse a channel, a new point one is formed. You can then take the swing low (point 2) and subsequent swing high (point 3), to form a new channel in the opposite direction. Refer to the figure below. Once you get comfortable with this technique you will know how to determine the trend in security. You will also know where the price "should go" if the security acts the way all securities have historically acted.

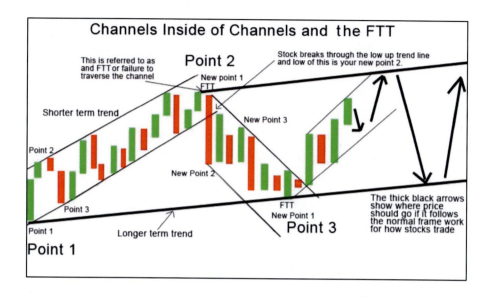

Price Gaps

A gap in a stock chart occurs when the opening price of a stock is above the previous day's closing price. These are most defined on daily or weekly charts however gaps occur in almost all asset classes and time frames. The reason that a gap occurs is because the market maker must adjust the stock price to meet the current supply or demand for a stock. When a market is closed and a news item or another catalyst impacts a stock, people will sometimes enter the market on open orders. These type of orders are executed at any price that a market opens at. If a number of these orders are in queue the market maker will increase or decrease the price of a stock, to reflect this added demand or supply. This causes a stock to gap up or down. Gaps are very pronounced in OTCBB and Pink sheet stocks since these exchanges are not open for after-hours trading when earnings and other news releases are usually released. Gaps are less pronounced in big board stocks since these stocks allow for electronic trading in the premarket (8:00-9:30 AM EST) and after-hours U.S. trading sessions (4:00-8:00 PM EST), however, they are certainly present. The volume is usually way above average when gaps occur however a stock can also gap up on below average volume. Gaps that occur on low volume usually fill quickly.

One thing to remember about penny stocks is that most gaps get filled within the first few hours of trading. What this means is that the price will drop back down to fall in line with the closing price of the candlestick that formed prior to the gap. This is called a "gap fill" and I would estimate it occurs 99% of the time within 1-5 days. Occasionally gaps remain unclosed for months or even years, however, this usually only occurs in big board stocks. GOOG is one stock that still has an unfilled gap in the $80-100 range, even though the stock now trades at $600. This gap probably will never be filled but ABC penny stock which gaps up from $0.25 to $0.65 due to a stock promotion, will almost always come back down and fill the gap in a week or less (usually 2 days). Remember that it is always a good idea to sell a stock that gaps a significant amount in your favor, as close to the market open (9:30:05) as possible. When a penny stock gaps a significant amount it sometimes will fill the gap in the first 5-30 minutes of the day. If the gap does not fill, there is a chance the stock could move higher without filling the gap, but this not very likely. See the figure below.

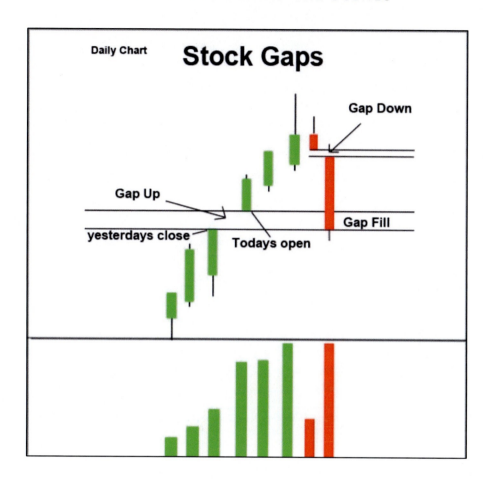

CHAPTER 3

CHART PATTERNS

C hart patterns form in all asset classes and in all time frames. Any time you look at a security such as a stock there is a good chance it is currently forming some sort of pattern. I am not explaining these patterns in order for you to trade off of them necessarily--except for maybe the breakout patterns, because there are thousands of books available that will explain these same patterns--but rather to give you an understanding of what other market participants may be looking for and how you can potentially take advantage of them. Once you can identify these patterns, you will have a better idea of how to potentially take the opposite side of the trade. Usually, the chart patterns play out the way the technical analysis books say they will, but they do so in a way that will prevent as many people as possible from taking part in the price movement. This occurs because most people are unable to deal with the volatility caused by failed breakouts. I have tried my best to explain most of these patterns from the perspective of buyers and sellers that are involved in these stocks.

Classic Breakout Pattern:

When a stock breaks above a resistance or support level, this is referred to as a technical breakout or breakdown. Sometimes it takes multiple attempts for a stock to breakout so it is usually better to wait until at least the third or fourth attempt before entering a trade, even if you are tempted to buy on the first or second attempt. When a breakout occurs, buyers flood into a stock pushing it higher. Once resistance is broken, there are no longer many sellers to hold the stock down and the stock should quickly rise or fall to the next resistance or support level fairly quickly, provided the volume is high. If the stock is at an all-time high, then there is no resistance and the price will increase rapidly. This type of buying is referred to as momentum buying and it is very important to try to buy when momentum is coming into a stock. This ensures that the stock will move up in the correct direction initially reducing your risk. When the stock pulls back to retest the breakout price level, you do not want the stock to drop below your entry price. If it does drop below you, want to see the stock spike back above very quickly or else it may be time for you to exit. If you miss a breakout, it makes more sense to wait to see if the stock comes back down to test the break level rather than chasing the stock above the breakout price.

In general, it usually takes two or more attempts for a stock to breakout. The longer the time frame of the resistance level and the more failed attempts that there have been to break this level, the stronger the breakout will be when it finally occurs. On a closing basis (not just intra-bar) I have found that a stock needs to move above the breakout price level by approximately 14.6% of the range of the consolidation zone. For example, in the figure below the high of the consolidation range was $1.50 and the low was $.75. If you multiply the difference by 14.6%, you get what I refer to as a breakout buffer zone of $.11.

What this means is if the stock breaks out and can't form a candlestick that closes above \$1.61, the breakout will typically fail. See the figure below for an example of a classic breakout. One thing to note is that this breakout occurred on the second attempt. This used to be a more common pattern but today stocks rarely breakout on the 2nd attempt. If you buy a breakout like this, you can expect a potential failed breakout more often than not, prior to the real breakout. If a breakout does work on the first attempt and a measured move target is hit, based on the range of the consolidation zone, you can expect a swift pullback to the breakout level once the uptrend line is penetrated. Note the stock will usually put in a double top pattern (which will be explained later in the chapter) before the pullback occurs.

Anatomy Of A Breakout:

Below are possible outcomes for a breakout or a breakdown and decisions that you will have to make. Therefore, you should have a plan in place to answer these questions when trading:

1. A stock breaks out of a range and you enter the stock. What do you do if the stock drops back into the initial range?

Answer: If it has attempted to breakout three times or more times and has failed, you should quickly exit the trade, take a small loss and wait for the next setup to occur. If the stock is trying to breakout on its fourth attempt, you're stop-loss should be moved up to a few cents below the 61.8% retracement level of the range that it broke out of. Stocks that try to breakout on their fourth attempt usually experience significant breakouts and therefore if a stock retraces more than 61.8% after this many attempts, there is a good chance that the breakout will be a failure.

2. If a stock breaks out of a trading range and you enter the stock and then the stock reverses and moves back across the prior range taking out your stop-loss, What should you do if the stock moves back into the range?

Answer: Regardless of how confident you are in your trading method, this type of outcome is bound to happen from time to time, and you must just remain disciplined, and take the loss when the stock hits your stop-loss. Next you should wait for a new trading range to form before you consider entering the stock again.

3. If a stock breaks out of a range and you enter the stock, and then the stock reverses and moves back across the entire range taking out your stop-loss, and continues to move in the opposite direction of the original breakout, what should you do?

Answer: This is a breakout failure. When this occurs, there is a very good chance a stock will continue to move in the opposite direction of your initial entry and, for this reason, you should immediately take the loss when your stop is breached. You could also reverse your position if short selling is part of your strategy. Remember to calculate new profit targets and place a new stop-loss as well.

4. A stock breaks out of its trading range and then moves in your favor but never reaches your initial target. What should I do?

Answer: If your initial target is never reached there is a chance that a stock may experience a false breakout. If a stock has been in a range for on average 25 or more bars (regardless of the time frame), breaks out and then fails to continue higher, you should quickly exit the trade. If the stock has gone your way by a decent amount and then it retraces more than 50% of the amount that it has gone in your favor, you should exit quickly. If a stock is going your way and then retraces more than 38.3%, you should tighten your stop to a few cents below the 38.3% retracement level and exit if that level is breached. If a stock is going your way and then retraces 38.3% but moves back in your favor, you should leave your stop just above the 38.3% retracement level. If a stock is going your way and then retraces 38.3% but then moves back in your favor and then retraces 38.3% again, (essentially forming a double bottom pattern) you should leave your stop just below the 38.3% price level and exit immediately if the short-term 38.3% retracement level is breached.

5. If a stock breaks out of its trading range and moves in your favor, eventually hitting your target exit price, what should you do?

Answer: You should exit the trade immediately. Considering this is exactly what you had hoped would happen there is no reason you should deviate from your initial plan. Doing so is very dangerous and on average will cause you to lose money over the long-term. Because of greed, it takes discipline to stick to your profit target especially since a stock could continue in your direction a significant amount after you exit. Regardless you must just be thankful your target was reached and move on to the next trade. Learning to do this is one of the main steps towards achieving consistent profitability which 95% of people have never learned to do.

Three Or More Point Breakout:

The 3 point breakout is typically referred to as a cup and handle pattern when the bottom consolidation phase forms a rounded shape, although the bottom does not always have to be rounded. In the figure below notice how the stock failed to breakout on the second attempt but broke out on the third attempt. This pattern is much more commonly seen after the classic breakout pattern fails and a third attempt at a breakout ensues, after a pullback to a Fibonacci level. This is a continuation pattern where the stock is in an uptrend, it pulls back, consolidates and then breaks out again. You should realize that sometimes these cup and handle patterns fail. The reason for this is because traders take the opposite side of the trade and short the stock after the formation of handle seems to be failing. Keep in mind most of the techniques found in basic technical analysis books today will cause you to lose money if you try to follow them exactly as stated. For this reason, give the pattern time to form, give it more leeway to play out and be careful to cut losses quickly if the breakout fails. To project where the stock is headed after it breaks through resistance at point 3 take the high at point 1 ($.42) and subtract the support level at ($.31), to get your target of at least ($.51). The stock could move higher but not before it pulls back when it hits the target price. Also, note that after the breakout the former resistance point almost always is tested to see if support will hold.

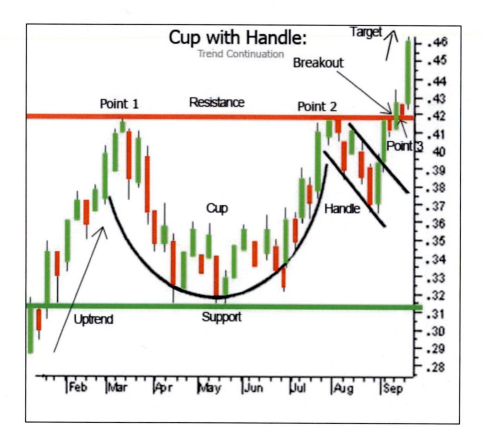

Bottom Reversal Breakout Pattern:

In general low price penny stocks have large run ups in their price per share over a short period of time, crash 30-50% and then slowly fade back down to the where they started. Eventually all of these stocks will bottom out and bounce a little as the dip buyers try to "catch a falling knife." The short sellers that caught the top will get scared that they will lose their profits, so they buy to cover pushing the stock higher. The stock will top out as the dip buyers take their profits and the stock will fall back to retest the support level on low volume in order to shake out the stubborn buyers that did not sell on the bounce. The stock will once again find support and the dip buyers will come into the stock again, causing the volume to spike and the price to rise. When the stock approaches the previous minor swing high, breakout buyers will enter the stock causing increased volume. This time, the stock will break above the high of the last bounce and more long-term short sellers will cover their positions, causing the stock to spike up to the former support level, which will now act as resistance. The smart dip buyers will notice the resistance and take their profits. Short sellers will also re-enter the stock when they realize the buyers cannot push up the stock any further. The stock will quickly fall back down to test the previous support level but once again the selling volume will dry up. A decrease in the selling volume will cause dip buyers to once again buy the stock, which will push the price up again. Short sellers will also once again look to cover their positions to take their profits or avoid a loss. Usually, if a stock cannot break through a support level on the third attempt, there is a good chance a bottom may be in place. The stock will approach the previous resistance level and breakout buyers will try to enter the stock again. This time, the stock may breakout a little, but the breakout will quickly fail as the dip buyers take their profits. Next the short sellers will once again attack the stock thinking that the stock may have put in a double top. The stock will fall but the buyers will come in more quickly, this time, only allowing for the stock to retrace 38% or 50% of its previous range from the support level where the stock bottomed, to the intermediate resistance level. This time buyers will realize that the stock is merely pulling back to a Fibonacci level and they will support the stock causing it to move back up. When the stock approaches the previous resistance level, it may have one more day where it pulls back a little or an intraday pullback where the stock drops in the morning to scare out the breakout buyers and gets bought up quickly. Either way the stock should not drop much and usually will close strong near the top of its range. The following day the breakout buyers will enter the stock again pushing it higher. When the stock breaks through resistance on the third or fourth attempt, shorts will quickly look to cover and a large short squeeze will occur as the volume rises to its highest level in a while. After the first breakout day, the stock will typically retest the former resistance level, which should now act as support. If support holds you'll want to place your stop below that support level or someplace around the 50% to 61.8% retracement level of the range on the day, the stock broke out. Your first target should be to sell 1/2 or 2/3 of your position at the next intermediate resistance level and then your stop-loss level should be moved to breakeven on the remaining shares. The second target should be the next major support level. These patterns can take days or several weeks to play out so you have to be patient, although they also form on intraday charts as well. They work best on stocks in the $.50 and up range.

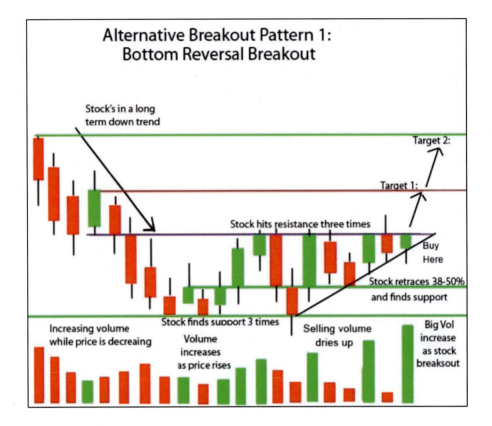

Alternative Breakout Pattern 1:
Bottom Reversal Breakout

Stock's in a long term down trend

Target 2:

Target 1:

Stock hits resistance three times

Buy Here

Stock retraces 38-50% and finds support

Increasing volume while price is decreaing

Stock finds support 3 times

Volume increases as price rises

Selling volume dries up

Big Vol increase as stock breaksout

Breakout Continuation Pattern:

A breakout continuation pattern occurs when a stock is in a strong uptrend and then starts to spike up on heavy volume. Buyers are in control and short sellers are getting squeezed hard. The stock will usually experience a large price increase in a short period of time. Eventually, buyers will start to dry up as the stock runs into some resistance. The stock will start to top out and a new set of short sellers will attack the stock. The stock will have a sharp sell-off but will quickly find support as dip buyers that missed the big run up look to buy the stock. The stock will usually retrace 50% to 76.4% of the range that it declined from the high to the low on the pullback, as the shorts that caught the top cover their positions. Soon the stock will run into resistance and short sellers that missed the top will be interested in shorting the stock. When the stock breaks below the previous bottom, the buyers stop-loss orders will be triggered and another leg down will occur. More shorts will enter the stock and the stock will move even lower, but the selling volume will eventually dry up. When the stock retraces 50 to 61.8% of the original range that it move up during the previous big run up, from the swing low to the swing high, buyers will once again enter the stock and cause the stock to bounce. This bounce will cause earlier short sellers to take profits and late shorts to cover in order to prevent losses. The stock will rise a little, but will drop back down as the support level is retested, in order to shake out the early round of buyers. If the support level holds the stock will quickly rise back up to the former support level which will now act as resistance. When a stock gets too far ahead of itself in a short period of time, it will usually experience a quick pullback and the dip buyers will probably take their profits. More short sellers will enter the stock and push it lower, but the stock will only retrace 38.3% - 50% of its range from the swing low at the support to the swing high at resistance. Now you can draw an up sloping trend line support level under the two higher low price levels. When dip buyers see that the sellers cannot push the stock lower they will enter the stock once again pushing the stock back towards resistance. When the stock hits resistance a few dip buyers may take their profits causing a one day or intraday pullback, but the sellers dry up quickly and the stock will close strong. When the stock approaches the resistance level on the 3rd or 4th attempt, it will most likely breakout as buyers enter the stock. You'll want to enter the stock at this time if the volume spikes. After the stock moves up a little, it may pullback to test the former resistance which should now act as support. This break of resistance is a key point and it will most likely trigger short sellers stop-loss orders causing a big spike in the stock, that will push the stock back up towards the swing high. Since many foolish buyers bought the stock before the big decline occurred at this price level, this level may be difficult to breakout above because all of these people will be eager to sell the stock in order to breakeven. For this reason, you will want to sell 1/2 or 2/3 of your position right around this resistance level. The stock will most likely pullback as smart people take their profits, but this time, it should not drop more than 38.3 to 50% of its range from the breakout point to the major resistance level at the high. If the stock finds support people that missed the first breakout will look to enter the stock. This should push the stock back to resistance. The stock may immediately breakout above the highs or pullback for a day as a few more people take profits, and the market makers try to scare buyers out of the stock. When the stock breaks above the major resistance on increased volume, the breakout buyers will jump back into the stock. Short sellers will most definitely place their stop-losses above a strong resistance level like this and once penetrated, a large short squeeze will occur. Your 2nd target to sell your remaining shares should be calculated by taking 23.6-50% of the difference between the major resistance level and your buy price at the previous breakout level, and adding this amount to the major resistance level. You should move your stop-loss up to a price just below the major resistance level. These trades can take days to several weeks to play out.

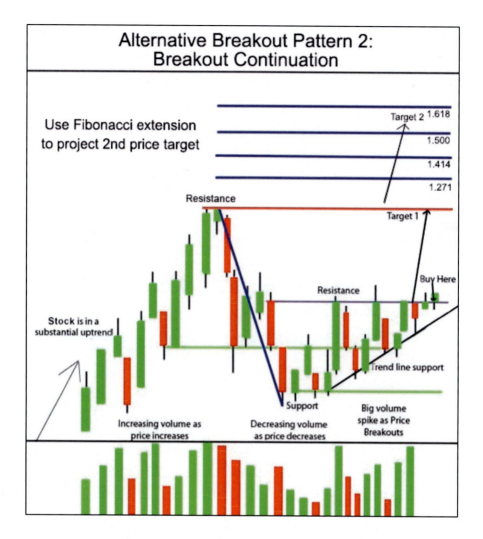

Double Bottom & Double Top Patterns:

The double bottom and double top patterns are some of the most common signs that a stock is most likely experiencing a change in trend. A double bottom pattern forms when a stock sells off due to an imbalance of sellers to buyers. Eventually, it reaches a support level where the sellers in the stock dry up and the buyers come in. When these buyers enter the stock, they start to push the price of the stock back up. In the process, short sellers may decide to cover their short positions pushing the stock up even more due to their persistent buying. Eventually, the buyers will dry up again and the stock price will stall usually at the 50% Fibonacci retracement level of where the initial sell-off point occurred. When this happens, short sellers may sense weakness in the stock and decide to re-short it. This will cause the stock to start dropping again which will scare out the buyers who thought it was going to return to its price before the initial decline. Buyers which were lucky enough to buy the stock near the bottom may decide to take their unrealized profits in fear of losing them. When they do this, the stock will start selling off again. When the stock returns to the previous low, there is a good chance that this point will act as a support level where buyers that missed out on the first rally will once again look to enter the stock. When this occurs the short sellers will again cover their positions pushing the stock up even more. When the stock gets back to a previous price level where the second sell-off occurred, this level will once again act as a resistance level and the stock might pullback again. Usually, on the second attempt, the breakout buyers will be stronger causing the stock to break through its resistance point. When this occurs, remaining short sellers will likely cover their positions potentially pushing the stock back up to where it started before the initial decline. Normally you would look to enter the stock when it finds support after the second sell-off or at the point where the stock breaks the resistance level from the first failed bounce attempt. If you take this trade, the target would be calculated by adding the difference between the resistance point and the support level, to the breakout level in order to project where the stock is most likely headed. The figure below is an example of a double bottom. Also, notice in the second double bottom figure there are multiple variations to this pattern.

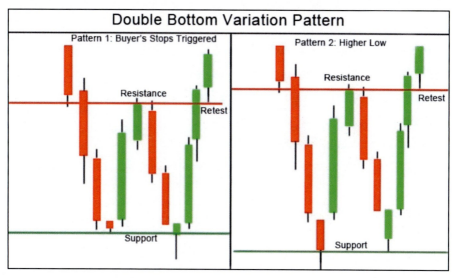

The double top is basically the exact opposite of the double bottom. A stock rally's because the number of buyers out-weighs the number of sellers. Eventually, the stock gets to a price level where the buyers start to dry up due to its high stock price. A good way to determine this is to see if the volume is increasing as the price increases. If it is not, you may be dealing with topping action in the stock. As short sellers sense weakness in the stock, they will usually attack causing the first pullback. As the stock dips, buyers may become interested in the stock again. When these dip buyers enter the stock, they will push the price higher causing the shorts to buy back their shares to cover their short positions. This will push the stock higher. As the stock approaches the previous high and the buyers once again start to dry up, sellers may start to come back to the stock again. If the buyers cannot get the stock to breakout above the high, short sellers may once again sense weakness and decide to short the stock. When this occurs, the stock will start to drop. When the stock drops to the support level, dip buyers that came in on the last pullback may be more reluctant to buy in fear that the stock will continue to collapse. As the stock breaks through the support level more, short sellers may enter the stock in hopes of pushing the stock lower. The stop-losses of dip buyers will most likely be triggered and a panic sell-off will occur. This is referred to as a breakdown, which is the opposite of a breakout. The target for the stock would be the difference between the previous high points, which is formed by the resistance level where the stock was not able to breakout and the support level where the stock broke down at.

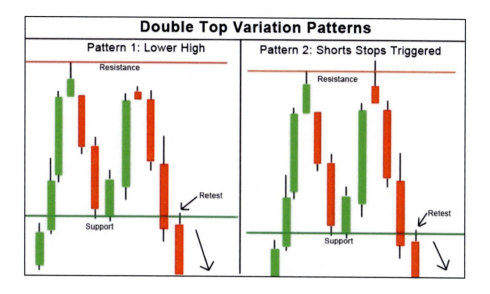

You can find these patterns in any asset class and in all time frames. The V Bottom reversal patterns that used to be common in the market are much less common today. You must expect to see one of these double bottom variation patterns anytime you expect a stock to reverse. Not all of these patterns work, but they usually are pretty reliable. Occasionally you will also see a triple bottom or a triple top but these are less common since stock usually breakout or break down on their third attempt at penetrating a support or resistance level. If you are buying penny stock pumps you need to be aware that these patterns will form quite frequently even on one minute charts.

Head and Shoulders Pattern:

The head and shoulders and inverse head and should patterns are fairly common trend reversal patterns. These patterns show up on all time frames and in all asset classes. They typical occur after a stock has rallied or sold off sharply and the stock is ready to reverse. A head and shoulders pattern occurs when a stock rallies to new highs and the buyers that have been pushing the stock higher eventually dry up. When aggressive short sellers see this topping action, they may look to short the stock. This will cause the stock to sell-off a bit. This selling pressure will cause current longs to sell their holdings due to fear of losing their profits. When this occurs the stock will pullback. After the stock retraces a certain amount, buyers that missed the run may look to enter the stock and lucky or smart sellers that sold near the top may also look to buy back the stock. When short sellers see this buying coming into the stock, some will quickly look to cover their positions, while others will use the previous high as their stop-loss. When the stock starts to get close to the resistance level, aggressive buyers may come into the stock anticipating a breakout. When the stock finally breaks out, even more, buyers will come into the stock. This excessive buying volume will most likely cause the short-sellers to cover their positions which will push the stock to new highs. Eventually, the buyers will once again dry up and the short sellers will re-enter the stock. This will cause the stock to pullback yet again. This pullback to the former resistance level will most likely act as a support level as buyers that missed the breakout will look for a second chance to buy. The stock price will start to rise again but this time, the buyers will not be strong enough to push the stock back to the high. When the short sellers sense the weakness and a lower high is formed, they will once again look to enter the stock and the stock will drop back to the support level. Since the second move higher has failed and the stock put in a lower high, buyers may be more apprehensive to defend the stock this time. For this reason, there is a good chance the stock will break through the support level triggering stop-losses. When this occurs panic selling will ensue and lots of short sellers will look to enter the stock anticipating a trend reversal. This forms the head and shoulders pattern. The target for a measured move would be resistance minus support subtracted from support at the neck line.

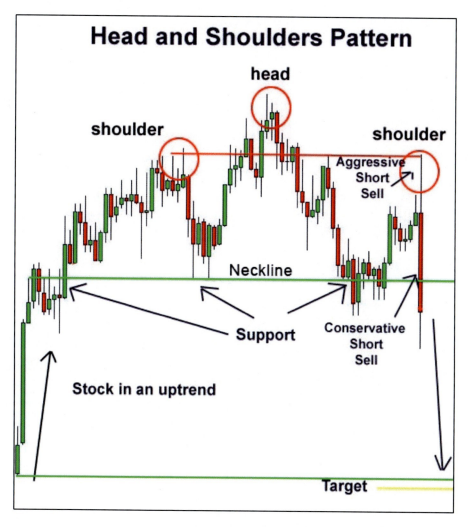

I am not going to cover the inverse head and shoulders pattern because it is exactly the same pattern as the head and shoulder's turned upside down so instead of shorting you would be looking to buy the stock. This is a very strong reversal pattern and occurs on all time frames. See figure below.

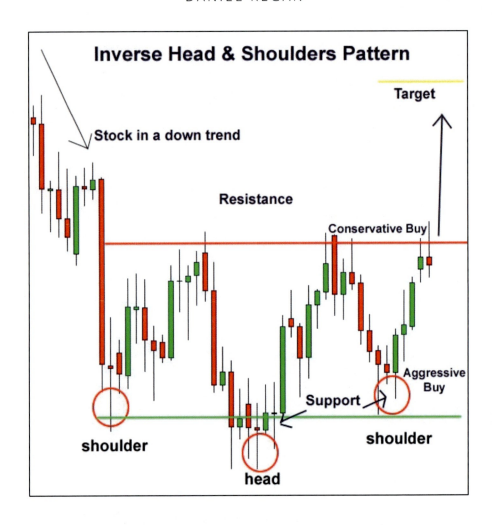

Continuation Patterns:

The triangle patterns are typically a form of trend continuation that show up constantly in all asset classes and on all time frames. There are way too many triangle related patterns to cover in this guide, but the basic idea behind the triangle pattern is that a stock is in an uptrend or downtrend, it experiences some congestion or consolidation and once it breaks through support or resistance formed during this congestion period, the trend continues. The most common types of triangle patterns are symmetrical, ascending, descending, pennants and flags. The figure below illustrates various triangle formations and the arrow shows where the pattern predicts the price should go (which usually occurs but not always). When a stock breaks out of one of these patterns, it will usually move at least as much as the widest part of the triangle pattern.

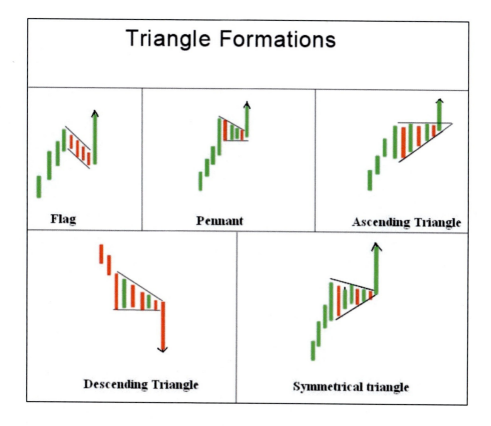

I wanted to give one real world example, so the next figure is a chart of a symmetrical triangle pattern. The target on this type of pattern when the stock breaks through support and resistance in the direction of the uptrend is measured by taking the high minus the low at the widest part of the triangle and projecting that distance above the breakout point. Normally a stock that breaks out of a triangle pattern

2/3 of the way through the formation will have a stronger move than a stock that breaks out closer to the apex where the two trend lines meet. Notice how the stock retests the trend line when it first breaks through it. This happens 99.9% of the time in all triangle patterns and occurs to shake people out, as well as to try to turn the former resistance level into a new support.

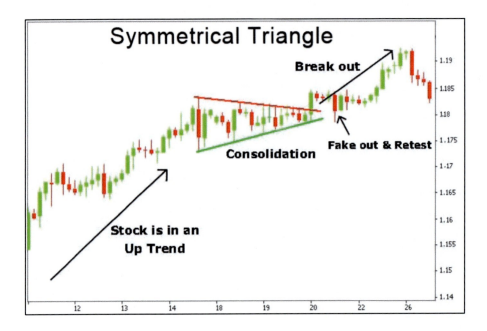

CHAPTER 4:

PSYCHOLOGY OF THE PENNY STOCK MARKET

95% Of Market Participants Lose?

It is a commonly held view that 95% of the people that take an active stance and try to time the market, lose money. About 4.0% of the people breakeven and 1.0% take all of the other people's money. In the penny stock market it is more likely 99.9% of people lose and 0.1% take everyone else's money. Trading is one of the hardest activities that you will ever do. It is not physically challenging, but at times will definitely test your mental state and sanity. The stock market is made up of millions of market participants that are trying to take somebody else's money whom is less informed. All these people analyze the same information and base their decision to buy or sell a security on this analysis. The fact of the matter is every trade that takes place has one buyer and one seller which means on any given trade one person wins and one person loses. If you want to make money, you will have to be more prepared than the person on the other side of your trade.

Most people look at the penny stock market like a casino. They throw a little money into it in hopes of hitting a jackpot. If they lose the money, it is not a big deal to them because a lot of the times it is just a few hundred or a thousand dollars. There are also very foolish people that take out home equity loans on their houses or mobile homes, in order to buy penny stocks that somebody told them will become the next AAPL stock or GOOG stock. These fools deserve to lose and this sort of situation happens quite frequently. It is these uninformed people whom we wish to take advantage of. If this basically describes how you were in the past do not worry because we are going to change this. It is actually legal to take their money, so why not?

Every once in a while, a random idiot gets very lucky and wins big in the penny stock market. This is equivalent to the guy your friend knows that won $25,000 from a slot machine and bragged to all of his friends or your coworker that won $18,000 from a scratch ticket. I believe the casino allows these sort of outcomes because by law they have to and the market does because they want the degenerates to keep coming back. If the average person never wins then people start to think the penny stock market is rigged (which it is) and then they will not continue to participate. This is bad for business so occasionally they allow some winners in order to entice more idiots. The general public fails to realize that there are professional traders, market makers and institutions like hedge funds, taking the other side of their trades. This group of people has better information and sometimes even inside information. They have much more capital than the average penny stock investor, which allows for them to withstand larger drawdown's and they trade in these stocks day in and day out. Every time they put on a trade, they know what the probability of the trade going their way is and will not risk their capital if they do not have some sort of a statistical advantage. They operate just like a casino and are considered to be "the house". Essentially you must try to be on the right side of the market with these guys or you have no chance to make money. While the right side in penny stocks is usually the short side, there are certain times when probabilities favor buying. My strategy focuses on these specific situations.

Fear & Greed:

Emotions are the root of all evil in trading. A trader that remains calm and can put their emotions aside, even in extremely stressful situations, will do well in the market. Fear and greed are the two biggest issues for market participants and they will make or break a trader. Although tiny amounts of fear and greed are important, most people let their emotions completely take control of their minds essentially causing an immediate defeat before the trade has even begun.

Fear causes people to skip trades they should have taken. It also causes people to sell their winners too early (because they think their profit will disappear if they do not) and hold on to their losers too long (because they cannot bear the thought of losing money on a trade they thought was a sure thing). These two issues will be described in the next chapter but they are very common and very bad for traders. Greed causes people to stay in a trade too long or chase a stock that has already moved past their planned entry price. Many people will tell you they are not greedy or the fear of losing money does not bother them, but in my experience this is not true. When the market dangles a whole weeks pay check in front of a person in five minutes, greed will overtake them. They will try to rationalize with themselves that they just want a little bit more than their initial target and in the end, will end up losing everything. This is a very common occurrence and for most people it is very difficult to overcome. At the same time when a person does not stick to their predetermined stop-loss and instead decides the stock will move back in their favor, the fear of losing is over taking them. A person must be disciplined enough to put these thoughts aside and act rationally, which is very difficult and counterintuitive for most people to do.

Taking Responsibility For Your Actions:

Taking responsibility for your actions is the only way to be successful in the market. If the chart pattern is in place, the stock has a catalyst that should cause it to move up in your favor, but instead it does exactly the opposite, how will you deal with this situation? Will you get pissed off and break your keyboard? Will you be foolish and average down? Will you get scared and sell immediately deviating from your original stop-loss? Realize that not all trades will work out and in fact, many trades will fail. You are the only person that can make a decision about whether to place a trade or not. There is no such thing as being "perfect" in the stock market. Perfection in the market means following your trading plan day in and day out even if that means losing 40% of the time. Psychologically this can be hard to deal with for most traders, but you must deal with this if you want to succeed in the market. Learn from your mistakes because losing is part of the learning process and losses are a cost of doing business in the market. Re-read this paragraph again because it is one of the most important in this guide.

Controlling Your Emotions:

As I mentioned earlier, emotions are a major hindrance to successful trading. The only way to avoid the negative outcomes caused by your emotions is to have a defined plan. Whether you create your plan ahead of time and it is fixed (i.e. a $.25 stop-loss and a $.50 profit target) or dynamic plan where the important variables change but everything else remains the same, it is important to realize that having a plan is one of the best ways to remain disciplined. People may claim to be successful at completely discretionary trading but from my experience very few people are able to make money consistently without a defined plan. You may want to take a position size three times what you normally would or change your stop-loss due to a sudden drop in the stock or chase a stock $.30 past your initial entry point, but if this is not in your plan, then there is no reason you should ever even consider these options. This type of behavior will most definitely cause you to lose all of your money. The fear and pain of losing your money and the greed and joy that comes from making lots of money will over power your rational thought process if you let your emotions cloud your judgment. Here is a link[1] to a great article on the market psychology of why the majority of people (the herd) buy high and sell low and thus lose money. I did not write this article but I suggest going to the website above and reading it.

---

[1] "Stock Market Psychology - Why We Buy High and Sell Low." Web blog post. *Hubpages*. Hubpages Inc., n.d. Web. 21 June 2012. <http://shibashake.hubpages.com/hub/Stock-Market-Psychology---Why-We-Are-Our-Own-Enemy>.

CHAPTER 5

MONEY MANAGEMENT

Protecting Your Capital:

S uccessful trading is based on managing your money properly. The only way for a trader to continue trading is if they learn to protect their trading capital. Without trading capital, you can no longer place trades and, therefore, it is equivalent to a company going out of business. Blowing up one's account--the process of losing all your money--is your number one goal to avoid. The way you do this is by never risking too much of your total account on any single trade. This gets to be more difficult when you start out with a small amount since you will only be able to buy a tiny amount of stock and, therefore, may have to hold longer to reach your higher targets. Losing $500 or 25% of your $2000 account in a penny stock trade gone wrong is not very difficult. Repeat this mistake four times and all of your money will disappear. It's not uncommon to occasionally experience four losing trades in a row. Now instead, imagine you started out with $50,000 in your account. Risking $500-1000 per trade is a lot easier and more realistic because this loss would only be 1-2% of your total account value. You would have to have 25-50 losing trades in a row to blow up and the probability of this is very low. Could it happen? Yes, anything is possible, but in trading, you have to go by the probabilities. Penny stocks are very volatile and extremely risky if not traded correctly. They can make extreme moves which could cause you to lose 50-75% of the capital that you put into a stock, in a matter of minutes and then reverse and come all the way back to where they were prior to the extreme move in a short period of time. Protect your capital, live to trade another day and eventually you will increase the value of your account.

Risk/Reward:

In any given trade the risk/reward ratio is the probability of success, versus the probability of failure. This is an extremely important aspect of managing one's trading capital in trading. Major support and resistance levels help us to calculate this ratio. In general, you want to be in a trade where the reward outweighs the risk by at least 2:1 (on average), but hopefully 3:1 or more. What this means is if on a specific trade you are willing to lose $1000, then your system must have a statistical edge that allows you to win $2000 or move on average on profitable trades. Essentially there must be positive expectancy that the trade will go in your favor and that your average profit will be at least twice the amount of your average loss or you won't make money in the long-term.

Win/Loss Ratio

To trade stocks successfully, you need a positive expectancy greater than 50%, which means you win more than you lose and your average winning trade must be bigger than your average losing trades. Stocks under $5 are non-marginable, so you cannot borrow money from your broker to trade these kinds of stocks. Therefore, you most likely need a positive expectancy and your average winning trade must be much larger than your average losing trade. For example, if you place 10 trades, 5 which are winners and 5 which are losers, your win-loss rate is 50%. This means 1 out of 2 trades will be a winner, so if you make $500 when the stock goes your way and lose $500 when the stock moves against you, after 10 trades you will be right back to where you started: (5 * $500 = +$2500 and 5 * $500 = -$2500 so your net profit is $0.00 minus commissions.) If your average winning trade is not larger than your average losing trade, then you will breakeven or lose a little due to commissions. Now if 8 of the 10 trades are in fact winners, the average winner does not need to be a lot larger than the average loser. For example, if your average winner is $500 and your average loser is $500, you would still make money: (8 * $500 = +$4000 profit and 5 * $500 = -$2500 loss, so your net profit is $1500). The problem with this is that is very difficult to win 80% of the time in the stock market. The more realistic win/loss ratio of a successful trader is 65% / -35% in stocks. In certain markets such as futures and currencies, you actually can make money with negative expectancy, for instance only winning 30% of the time. The reason this is possible is because of the inherent 10:1 or as much as 500:1 leverage, available in these asset types. Using the same example as before, if 3 of your trades are winners and 7 are losers, but your average win is much bigger than your average loss, you still will still make money: (3 x $3000 = $9000 profit and 7 x $500 = $3500. Net profit is $5500). Money management is extremely important to pay attention to because you cannot make money if you do not use it. I suggest reading a lot more on the subject.

Drawdown's:

A drawdown is the reduction in ones trading capital after a series of losing trades. Drawdown's are usually presented as the percentage of a person's trading capital that has been lost. Just because a trading system wins 80% of the time does not necessarily mean for every 100 trades, you will win the first 80 of them that you make. Unfortunately, there is no way of knowing which of the 80 out of those 100 trades will be winners. You could lose the first 20 trades in a row and win on the next 80 trades or win on the first 20, lose on the next 40 and then win on the final 20. If you do not size your position correctly, those 20 losing trades could potentially add up to a total loss that eliminates all of your trading capital. If this occurs, you will be out of the game for good or at least until they raise more capital. This is why money management is so important. No matter what type of trading you do, you will be guaranteed to face a losing streak at some point in time. The key to being a successful trader over the long-term is coming up with a trading plan that enables you to withstand these periods of losses. In a sense, this is exactly what the risk management parameters that I have detailed, will help you to do.

What is Risk?

Your risk on any given trade is in most cases the distance between your entry price and the next major support or resistance level. Since support and resistance levels are where buyers or sellers usually come into a stock and prevent the stock from going lower for longs or higher for shorts, it makes sense to define your risk by these levels. If buyers don't end up entering the support level will crack, short sellers will attack the stock and the price will most likely move to the next support level. If short sellers don't end up shorting the stock at resistance, the resistance level will crack, breakout buyers will enter the stock and the stock will move higher. Basically, you place your stop $.01 below a support level and if your entry price turns out to be wrong, your risk is considered to be your max loss (if you stick to your stop-loss price). The hard part about setting a stop-loss is that the market makers and traders know where people will typically place their stop-losses and they will normally try to move the market in a way so as to trigger peoples' stop-losses, steal people's money and then the stock will continue in its original direction. This typically happens around 12:00 or 1:00 P.M. when the volatility in the market is lower. You probably have experienced this exact situation where you enter a stock, it immediately goes against you and stops you out, only to reverse and move to the original target. You feel like the market is set up in a way to screw you out of your money and, in all honesty, this is true. The next time you may end up taking the trade without a stop-loss order and will end up losing twice as much. Getting stopped out of trades is no fun, but unfortunately, it is an inherent part of trading successfully. The best way to minimizing this is to use wider stop-loss orders and decrease your position size accordingly. Also, another way to manage risk is to look for the range (high minus low) of largest 5 minute candlestick on the 10 day chart of a stock that you want to trade and place your stop-loss just above the range of the largest candlestick. If the range is too large, then you should decrease your position size to reduce your risk or skip the trade altogether. Some people also like to use the Average True Range (ATR) indicator. This indicator takes the average range of a stock over X number of periods but takes into account stock gaps. The standard setting is 30. I like to use a period of 60 and when possible use 1.5*ATR's for day trades or 3.5*ATR's for swing trading.

Position Sizing:

Position sizing is very important part of trading. If you position size is too small in relation to your account size, you can win on a lot of trades, but your profits will not add up too much. If your position size is too large, one of your losing trades could cause you to potentially lose all of your trading capital, which means you no longer will be able to trade. For these reasons, you must carefully calculate the correct amount of money to risk on each trade. This is referred to as position sizing or sizing your position. For instance, if your account is $30,000 you should not risk the entire value of your account on a single trade because you are exposing yourself to far too much risk. This would completely violate the principles of proper money management. In general you should never place more than 10-25% ($3000 to $6000) of your equity in any one trade, 25% being on the extreme side. So assume you are interested in buying a $1.00 stock. First determine what nearest significant support level is. In this case, it is $.85. You will want to place your stop-loss $.01 below this at $.84 for a max risk of $.15 per share. Next you decide to risk no more than 2.0% of your account on any one trade ($30,000 * 2% = $600.) You may need to increase this amount to 5% if you have a small account. You would calculate the position size as: (Max dollar Loss / stop-loss size in dollars) = # of shares to buy: ($600/$.15) = 4000 shares. Since this value falls in line with your capital as a percentage of your total account value, this would be a proper position size assuming you stick to your stop-loss. If your account is much smaller, for instance, $5000, you probably will not want to use more than 40-50% in any one trade. This may seem like a large percentage, however as I said earlier if the amount of capital is too small the profits will essentially be nothing after commissions and slippage are factored in. Therefore, you will either will need to raise more capital or forget about trading profitably. While the chance of a halt, bankruptcy or some other negative news is possible at all times in these type of scams, which could cause a significant loss of capital, it is a risk you must take. Provided that you are not putting all of your money into any given trade, you will live to trade another day in the event of a catastrophe such as the 911 terrorist attacks, where the market was halted for 5 days and resulted in a large drop in all stocks. Trading with less capital is more difficult, but remember that *you never should be trading with money that you cannot afford to lose!*

Provided with this guide is an Excel spread sheet that I created that will calculate your position sizes automatically. The file is called **My Position Sizing Spreadsheet.xlsx**. The spread sheet will calculate the correct position sizes for various stock prices from for instance .$10 to $50.00 (using $.50 increments). I suggest you print it out and tape it to the edge of your monitor, so you can refer to it on every trade. Eventually, you will start to memorize the proper sized positions and this will make things easier. If your trades are planned out ahead of time, you will always be prepared with the proper position size, but if you end up taking news or alert based trades which can occur at any moment, you will be more prepared for this sort of situation as well.

Stop-loss Order's: Mental / Hard & Software Based:

A stop-loss order (mental or hard stop) is essential to limit your risk and keeping your losses in check. A stop-loss limit order guarantees that your stop-loss will only be placed at the limit price that you choose once your stop price is reached. Unfortunately, in a fast moving stock, there is no guarantee that your broker will be able to execute any or all of your position at this price which means it's dangerous to leave a stop-loss limit order unattended. A stop-loss or stop-loss market order will execute your position at the current market price once the stop-loss order price is hit. Unfortunately, there is no guarantee that when your order is actually executed the price will be anywhere near the stop price that you set. For these reasons, people in the OTCBB and Pink sheet markets usually choose not to use hard stop-losses placed with their brokers and/or the exchange. Instead, they tend to use mental stop-losses or software based stop-losses (stored on their broker's server only, not the exchanges) whereby they set a price that once hit will cause them to manually place an order to execute their order automatically. The problem with a mental stop-loss is whether you actually have the discipline to stick to your stop-loss and actually get at your mental stop price. If you are disciplined, a mental stop is the way to go when trading penny stocks, however, most new traders think they are disciplined when they really are not. OTCBB and Pink sheet stocks require you to sell into strength when the stock is still rapidly rising, in order for you to get your order executed. Once the stock starts to drop, it is too late to sell because there are literally no buyers and the market makers do not immediately have to post a bid price like in listed stocks. What this means is once one of these stocks starts to drop it is already too late to get out. Also, when you place a hard stop that is saved to the exchanges server, market makers can see your stop-loss order and if it is too close to the current price, they may try to run your stop-loss. This means they will buy or sell in an attempt to move the price in a way that will trigger your stop-loss so they can take your money. Then the stock will continue to head in its original direction. This can be very frustrating but it is part of trading. A mental stop-loss could end up getting triggered if you place it in an area where you would expect many other people to place their stop-losses, for example near the closest minor support level. I typically use software based stop-loss market orders if the stock is liquid enough or else I place a serious of stop limit orders all in a row so that my order is broken up into a much smaller size for instance 500 shares per order. This usually allows me to get out of a stock when I need to, however, I sometimes have to pay the commission for multiple trades. This is fine with me since I would rather pay $25 instead of potentially losing $2,000 due to severe slippage.

CHAPTER 6

MY TRADING RULES

Trading rules make up the basis for a person's trading plan. If you stick to the rules, you will most likely make money. If you break the rules, there is a large chance you will lose all your money. These rules are in no particular order, but all are very important to becoming a consistently profitable trader.

1. Never hold a losing position overnight.

I suggest never holding a position overnight unless you are up a sizable amount already on the trade (for example if you are already locked in a partial profit). The reason for this is that a lot of times a stock that has gone against you will gap in the same direction and continue to go against you. A small loser may turn into a larger loser and this is exactly what we are trying to prevent. If you have a margin of safety from locking in a partial profit prior to the close, then it may be okay to hold the remaining shares overnight, but if you are down $500 on a stock and it is not closing strong in the upper 5% of its trading range, it is usually not smart to hold overnight. I find the most profitable trades that I take are the ones that immediately show a profit from the start. I find when a stock goes against you by for example 10%, you need a 20% gain just to get back to even.

2. Never under any circumstance add to a losing position!

Unless you purposefully take a 1/3, 1/4 or 1/2 size position to "test the waters in a stock" and "get some skin in the game" because you are not sure whether you are properly timing your trade, there is no reason to ever average down in a losing trade that is just clearly going against you. The market makers have access to the limit book that shows the supply and the demand (which you never will have access to) and know the specific price levels where a large amount of buyers or short sellers enter the market. For this reason, when a stock you are long does not do what you expect and cracks through and closes below a major support level, you can be sure that the stock will not rise back to your entry price anytime soon. For instance, if you are long 1000 shares of a stock at $1.00, and the stock drops to $.50, and you decide to buy 1000 more to bring your average price down to $.75, when the stock rebounds as short sellers cover, you can be sure it will not go past $.75 before it continues to move lower. This means you either break even if you have the discipline to close the trade immediately (which most people do not) or your loss gets even larger as the stock takes out the support level at the low set at $.50 and moves to $.25. This occurs because the market makers know the way the average uninformed market participant thinks, and, therefore, the algorithms they use are set up in a way that will prevent you from making money. Average up on winners, but never average down on losers! When you average down and make money on a trade, you are essentially beating the odds and this rarely occurs.

3. Be patient with winning trades however extremely impatient with losing trades.

Sometimes trades take time to play out. Normally this occurs because the market makers do not want everyone making money. They know when a large amount of buying or selling volume hits a stock and what direction a stock will go, but they will sometimes hold the stock back trying to get impatient or bored people out of the stock. Do you ever find that you cut your loss in a stock and then a minute later it spikes up the way you expected it to? This is what is occurring when this happens. Losing trades are the complete opposite. If a stock does not do what you expect when you enter a trade, you do not want to give it too much time. If buying at support after a decline, the longer a stock goes sideways, the better the chance the market makers will at the very least let the stock crack through and trigger stop-losses. If a stock has true support, it will quickly bounce back above the support level, but if not, it will drop down to the next major support level. The longer you wait to cut your loss, the larger your loss will grow and grow it will. On the opposite side of the spectrum, if a stock goes sideways or slightly against you gyrating back and forth without hurting you, there is a good chance you have found yourself a winner. If the stock is going to go lower, it will usually happen quickly and you will immediately lose money.

4. Never let a major winning trade turn into a losing trade.

Although losses are a part of trading that cannot be avoided, what you can prevent is letting a winner turn into a loser. I am not referring to a $2.00 stock that you are up $.02 per share on, but rather when you have a substantial unrealized profit. If you are up $.50 on a stock and it suddenly reverses on you, there is no reason to let this trade turn into a loser. In these situations, you should always move your stop to breakeven, or even $.25 above your entry price. When you move your stop, it is also a good idea to sell part of your position and lock in a profit. If the stock falls back down you may lose some of your unrealized gains which is always an inherent risk when trading, but you will not lose your initial capital and you may even come out with a partial profit.

5. Always pay yourself at least partially on a winning trade.

It is a good idea to get in the habit of setting multiple target prices and sticking to them. Even if you expect a stock to rise to your final target, there is always a significant chance that you are wrong and some factor will prevent the trade from occurring the way that you expected. If you sell 1/4 or 1/3 of your position at predetermined price levels such as major resistance levels, moving averages or other technical levels, you increase the odds that if the stock reverses prematurely you will still come out with a winning trade or at least break-even.

6. Set your stop-loss order and stick to it.

While a hard stop-loss order is the best way to limit your losses and keep you disciplined, it is not always possible right when you buy into a penny stock. As soon as you have a decent profit in a penny stock it is good to set a stop-loss order assuming you are trading a liquid stock which you should be if you follow my method. This is only true if you are using software like Speedtrader's Das Pro which has a stop that the market makers cannot see due to the fact it is stored on your computer. Very few people can stick to mental stop-losses even though they think or claim they can. A lot of times when a stock starts dumping it is best to have a stop in place which will hopefully protect you. You most likely will not get out at the exact price you planned due to slippage considering nobody will want to buy an OTCBB or Pink sheet stock once it starts to dump, but it is better than nothing and the fact that you have planned to get out at a specific price will reinforce that it is imperative that you stick to your plan. I'd rather lose an extra 10% rather than 50% or 60%.

<u>7. Forget about trying to make money and instead, focus on trading your plan.</u>

When you trade, you should be trying to execute your trading plan. You should not be trying to make XXX amount of dollars per day, week, month, or year. It is best to not even look at your profit and loss when in a trade because profits and loss just instill fear and greed. If you follow the trading patterns and know what should happen, and what you will do if it does not, then you will be in a much better position to profit in the market.

<u>8.Once you have successfully traded a stock and earned a profit, remove that stock's ticker from your screen unless you are planning to trade the stock again.</u>

Many times traders get mad when they notice the stock they just sold for a $500 profit is now trading 50% higher a few minutes later. While it is no fun to think about the potential money that "could have been made" if you continued to hold the stock, it is a lot worse when the stock drops 50% on you because you were greedy and did not lock in your profit. For this reason, if you get out with a profit in a stock and do not plan to trade the stock again, just take it off your screen. This will allow you to focus on other stocks and prevent you from obsessing over it. Also do not say stuff like "I could have made 50% more if I did not sell so early." This primes your brain to change your plan which obviously is working correctly since you made a profit. The next time

111

you take a trade, you may try for 25% more and in the process lose 50%. Greed will destroy you!

9. Taking profits too early is one of the main ingredients to becoming consistently profitable.

Get used to the fact that if you are taking profits too early, but covering your losses by at least 2:1 (preferably 3:1 or even 5:1), you are on your way to profitability. You'll never be able to sell the top or pick the bottom exactly. You may get lucky sometimes, but most of the time you will hold your winners too long and cause a winning trade to turn into a loser. If you are earning an average profit that is larger than your average loss you are doing something right.

10. Do not chase a stock past your initial entry price plus or minus a small amount.

Short-term trading of stocks requires timing your entries correctly. Stocks that hit key price levels, or have some other catalyst, will usually experience a sharp move in a specific direction in a very short period of time. Once all of the buyers dry up, the stock will not rise for much longer and you could lose a lot of money very quickly if you chase the price past the initial entry, especially with penny stocks. If you miss your entry and do not expect a promotion to continue for multiple days, it is best to just pass on the trade.

11. If your order to buy is filled easily, run away immediately.

If it is easy to buy into a promoted stock (or any stock for that matter) at the start of the promotion when it should be very difficult, it is a sure sign that you should exit immediately. Anytime a penny stock is going to rise, you will have a very hard time getting your orders executed, even using market orders. The same is true for your sell order. If you are able to sell a stock easily, then there is a good chance that a stock is going much higher. Testing a 100-500 share order may be your best way to determine whether the odds are in your favor or not. Do not worry about paying the $5.00 commission because this little tactic could save you a lot of money. In the case of the alerts by the premier promoters, you will not have to worry about testing the stock when buying as long as you are trading within a couple minutes of when the initial alert is released. When selling your shares, it may be a good idea to test a small sell order.

CHAPTER 7

MY TRADING METHODOLOGY

In order to make money in the market consistently you must utilize a strategy or method which has a statistical edge. A statistical edge does not mean you make money every trade. This is impossible and the trading guru's that sell their worthless trading systems for thousands or tens of thousands of dollars love to feed off these people that believe this fallacy. They are in search of a holy grail trading system that never posts a losing trade and can turn you into a millionaire in two weeks. Unfortunately, there is no such thing and there never will be because as I said earlier, the market is a series of probabilistic outcomes! You may get lucky here and there without an edge, but you will not make money over the long-term and eventually you will lose all of your money. A statistical edge is having a method of stock selection and entry and exit prices that consistently allows you to extract profits from the market over the long-term. Money management also plays a large role in this because there is no way to profit if you do not keep your losses small and allow your profitable trades to offset your losses by more than a 1:1 ratio. When you combine technical analysis, trading rules, money management and trading psychology, you end up with a trading plan.

Opt-In Email Pumps:

Besides my technical trading system that I use to trade various asset classes such as stocks, bonds, forex, futures and options, my edge when trading penny stocks is to follow the pump emails that I receive from specific stock promoters. Please be aware these emails are becoming less important now that the promoter Awesome Penny Stocks has been shut down, but there still are some opportunities. Opt-in email penny stock promotion websites allow you to subscribe to their stock picking newsletters for free. I am a subscriber to over 600 free stock promotion websites online and included with this book is a copy of an Excel spread Sheet, which has my current website list and any known website connections. There is a good chance that there are more sites that I have not found yet, including fee-based stock promotions sites (which are useless), but I try to keep up to date with new additions when I find them. You will want to do the same as well in order to grow your list. You can find new sites by checking for advertisements on the search engines, as well as searching for key words like penny stock using Google. What most people do not realize is that many groups of these websites are operated by the same company or person/stock promoter. By having multiple websites, these stock promoters can build a large list of email addresses which they can use to send out their stock promotion campaigns. The more people that subscribe to their sites, the higher the stock price will spike when they release their stock promotions.

Creating A Pump Email Account:

I created a new Gmail account specifically for receiving these penny stock promotion emails. The name I use is Sentstocks1@Gmail.com. Choose a name that has nothing to do with spam or some of the websites will not let you sign up (don't use something like "spamstocks@gmail.com"). The reason that I signed up for this email account is because I receive thousands of emails from these websites every week and I would not want these emails coming to my personal email address. In order to track promoters, I set up labels in my Gmail account so that I can find out which sites the promoters are using. These labels allow me to archive all the emails I receive which basically gives me a database of every pump email that the promoters send out. By having this information, I can put in a specific ticker symbol into the Gmail search box to see whether it has ever previously been pumped. I can also click on a label to see every email that has been sent out by a specific promoter which allows me to research the time of day they usually release their alerts or how long their promotions last.

These email labels are included in a Word file called **"Stock Promotion Email Labels.doc."** You should setup 1 Gmail accounts strictly for receiving pump emails from the promoters. After you do this, you should open the excel spread sheet that I provided called **"Stock Promotion Website List.xlsx"** and start signing up for each stock promotion website using your new Gmail accounts. If any of the websites ask for a name, just use a random name (I use the name Cletus Vandamn personally). It will take a while to sign up for all these websites, but it can be worth the effort. If you double click the web address in Excel it should open the promoters website in your browser. Please understand the promoters come and go quite frequently so the list does change. If the list seems outdated don't worry, just skip the links that do not work or feel free to contact me at support@beatstockpromoters.com and I may have an updated version of the spreadsheet. In recent months, the penny stock market has been less active so I suggest spending time learning how to read charts and the way stocks trade and then you can focus on building your pump email account when you have a better understanding.

Next you will want to login to your first Gmail account. You will need to open the first email sent by each of the stock promotion website and make sure to click the link to confirm your membership if there is a confirmation link. Note some websites will not have a confirmation links. Also, make sure to check you spam folder for these confirmation links and if you find any, mark them as "not spam." After you do this, click on the little **"gear icon"** in the top right corner of your Gmail account and choose **" settings."** On the menu bar at the top click on **"Filters."** Next click on where it says **"Create a new filter,"** then open the Stock Promotion Email Labels.doc file and select the first emails (*@stocktips.com) and copy this into the box that is labeled **"Filter From:"** in your Gmail account. Now click where it says **"Create filter with this search >>,"** and if a box pops up that says: "Your changes have not been saved. Discard changes?" choose **"OK."** Now click the check box next to where it says **"Star It:"** and **"Never send it to spam".** Next click the check box next to where it says "**Apply the label:"** and then click the arrow for the drop-down menu and select: **"New label..."** Where it says: "Please enter a new label name:" enter: **Stocktips.com.** Now click on **"Create."** You have now created your first label. Repeat the process above for all of the labels in the Stock Promotion Email Labels.doc file. You can set up all of the secondary stock promoter and unknown connections websites, the same way but don't check the box to star them since you only want to place a star next to the important emails that you receive. Notice that certain email labels have *@ in front of the domain name. I did this because sometimes promoters will send emails from various email addresses. The *@ before the domain tells Gmail to apply a filter to any email received from a specific email address. Also, when you want to add email addresses for new stock promotion websites that you find, just use OR with a space on either side. This will apply your label to any website to you input into the From box under Create new filter in Gmail settings.

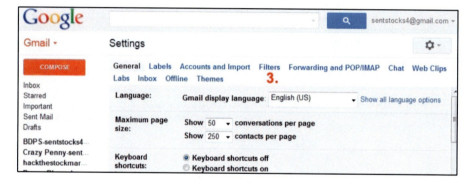

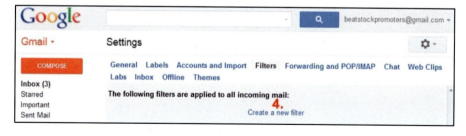

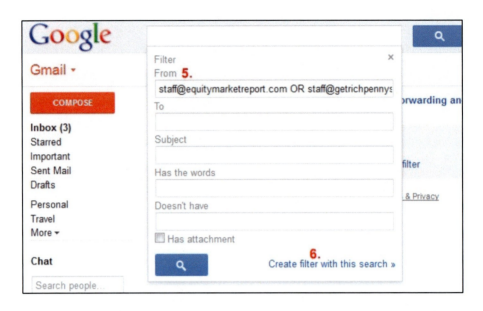

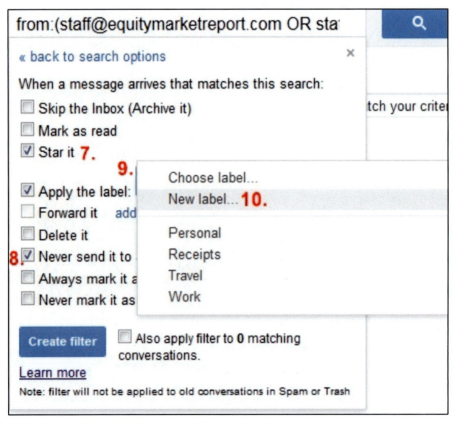

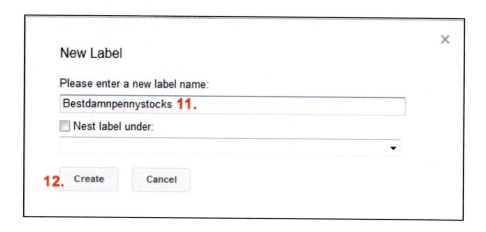

Please note the images are for display purposes only and are not showing stocktips.com

Once all the labels are created and everything is setup, every email you receive from one of the twenty Bestdamnpennystocks websites will be starred and labeled in your inbox and will never be sent to your spam folder. Make sure next to where it says "Try on a new inbox" to click on "starred first" so that the starred premier promoters emails will show up at the top of your email account window ahead of the less important emails. After you have viewed an email, you will need to click the check box or the box at the top to check all emails and then choose archive. You can delete emails from the secondary promoters or the unknown connections but always archive emails from the premier promoters. All of the emails that you give a label to and then archive will be saved under the labels in the left column of your Gmail account so you can refer back to them as needed.

Knowing these connections can tell you if you should exit a current trade in one of these promoted stocks or stay in the trade longer. When the promoters stop sending emails it is a crystal clear sign that the promotion is over and you do not want to own one of these scam stocks when the music stops unless you don't mind losing 50% of your money in a few minutes! Pump emails usually stop as soon as a pump and dump starts to crash. Occasionally a promoter may send out emails after a stock has already crashed in order to cover themselves in case the authorities come after them. This makes it look like they are still promoting the stock even though their third party client has already dumped their stock.

Emails Used To Inflate The Price

The way that stock promoters help to increase the price of these worthless penny stocks is through their persistent flow of pump emails. Besides bogus news releases, pure technical trading patterns and other news related items, the only other way that penny stocks go up are through stock promotions. In order to get the price of a stock to rise stock, promoters will stagger the interval of time when their various groups of their subscribers will receive their emails. Sometimes I will receive emails from a promoter's various websites every few minutes and other times they may try to spread out their emails over a number hours or even days. They do this to try to cause multi-day spikes in the price of a stock which is more difficult to do and, therefore, less common. When clueless people receive the emails from these sites at different times, they will enter market orders and the stock price will seem to go straight up with no major pullbacks. Smart traders can profit off these opportunities but there are much less of them than there was a few years ago.

Many websites only send emails while the market is closed however a few websites only release alerts while the market is open. The reason for this is because they want to make a stock gap up at the open so that the third party can sell a bunch of stock at higher prices, to unsuspecting idiots that think the stock is going to increase in price by 10000%. Alternatively, they may choose not to do this in order to try to get the stock price to run up much more over multiple days, so that they can sell millions of shares at higher prices.

Stocks that gap up almost always come back down and "fill the gap" before they have any chance to go higher but the second tier promoters almost never can keep a stock up for more than a few minutes to a couple hours at most. For this reason, you never want to buy a penny stock that gaps up more than 10-25% unless it consolidates for several hours or days, at or above the gap price which is extremely rare for a promoted penny stock. The exception to this rule would be if a stock gaps up due to a pump email which is sent while the market is closed by one of the premier promoters. In this situation since nobody could front load a stock, I would be willing to buy it even if it has gap up 50-100%, but only under one circumstance. In this case my strategy would be to use a broker that allows premarket trading such as Interactive Brokers, Speed Trader, or Center Point Securities to purchase the stock in the premarket around 8 A.M EST. I only would do this if I noticed some bigger blocks were trading in the stock in the premarket. This doesn't happen often but once in a while you can catch a stock early and be one of the first people to sell into the idiots and fools that are chasing the stock at the market open or within the first 15-30 minutes of the trading day. In the first 5-15 minutes these stocks should be liquid enough to take a large position and get in and out fairly easily.

"Premier" Stock Promoters:

Out of the 600+ stock promotion websites that I track only a small number of promoters (less than 10-20 websites in total) have stock picks that could be worthy of buying and the amount of good promoters continues to drop constantly. The fact is a lot of the volume that used to trade in the penny stock market has now flowed over into the small cap penny stocks instead. The average person may look at the OTC markets and think nothing has changed from a few years ago, but the reality is that this is not the case. With that said there still are opportunities, just not nearly as many. I have given the premier promoter the following specific title to help identify them. The #1 promoter in the world right now is Finest Penny Stocks. The currently have 26 domain names that they are using to build their email lists for promoting their chosen penny stock pump and dumps.

The main reason this promoters has been successful is because they have built up an email list with hundreds of thousands or even millions of people. They also pay millions of dollars to the search engines for PPC (pay per click) marketing in order to get their websites to be viewed by millions of people and place ads on heavily viewed websites like Yahoo Finance. They also release their alerts differently from the rest of the other promoters and their stock promotions budgets are typically several hundred thousand or even millions of dollars, instead of $1,000 to $100,000 like most of the secondary stock promoters.

Smallcapfortunes.com used to be a premier promoter but unfortunately they not successful anymore. Their most successful past pumps were FCPG, HHWW, ALZM, KNKT, but their last decent pump was in AAVC several years ago, and that one prematurely crashed due to a dilutive financing on the first day of the pump. They also had a number of failed pumps such as TKDN. Lebed is another promoter which used to be successful but I would not consider him one of the top promoters since most of his paid promotions with $20,000 in compensation per pump, have been unsuccessful. With a partnership between his site Inflation.us and Wallstreetgrand.com, he has done well pumping OPTT, BVSN, and SYNC. These stocks are all real company's and Lebed claimed that he was not compensated for the stock promotions. He has sent out strictly email pumps and in the disclaimer he disclosed his "clients position" which is usually a multi-million dollar amount, in the stock he is alerting. He also claimed that they would be holding the stock due to a lock-up period and will not sell until a specified date. They have taken massive positions in these stocks that they have alerted and the prices have dramatically increased but usually only for 1-3 days which is why I only trade them right when a promotion is released. Lebeds own website lebed.biz is no longer active. You need to make sure that the disclaimer to his email alerts states no monetary compensation and that his client owns a substantial stake in the company. Please ignore all other emails from him because this promoter seems to send 10+ per day.

Finally, the last four promoters had at least one or more successful pumps in the past several years. They are: STEV/STVF Pumper, EMBA pumper Their promotions have lasted several days to a few weeks. The stocks have run from the $.20 range all the way up to $1.00, $2.00 or even the $3.00 per share range. People usually find the stocks that they alert on prior to the pump using a trade count or unusual volume scanner. If you trade their pumps hold for a few days at most and watch the volume. Use a 15% stop-loss and try to sell into a gap up or a midday spike. A relatively new promoter to the scene recently pumped GNIN. This was a very successful promotion so it would be a good idea to keep an eye on their future promotions. Their site is called www.todayspickis.com, and they were able to move a stock from $.50 to 3.20 in 3 weeks!

Secondary Stock Promoters:

The reason I keep track of so many stock promotion websites and add any new ones I find, (just contact me at support@beatstockpromoters.com if you ever want the updated list) is because occasionally the premier stock promoters will pay some of these secondary promotions sites to pump their alerts. Also, sometimes the secondary promoters send out copycat alerts to their email lists with the same tickers that the premier promoters are pumping. They do this to try to piggy back off the premier promoters because they know how successful their alerts usually are. Secondary promoters can be useful if you are in a trade where the premier promoter has already released the alert to all of their email lists. You will know if you still have a bit more time to exit the stock since some new suckers will see the secondary stock promoters pump emails and may look to buy the stock. Never the less, most of these secondary promoters only release alerts when the market is closed and these type of alerts are almost always useless (and potentially dangerous) due to the typical gaps that they cause unless you are already in the stock from the previous day.

I am not saying that it is not possible to make money off them because the stocks that certain secondary promoters alert on sometimes go up 10 to 100%, but, in general, they are not consistent and the volume is typically pretty low. This makes it nearly impossible to take a decent size position and very difficult to sell when you want or need to get out. Some of the better secondary stock promoters are: Appeal, Alley, Beacon Equity, SpeculatingStocks, The500pct.com and Nitrox (the new kids on the block). There are many other groups of stock promotion websites but these are the main secondary ones. You definitely should have your Gmail account that you use for receiving the pump emails open and visible to you at all times while you are watching the market because alerts can come at any time of the day. Please understand secondary promoters are becoming more and more irrelevant each day so use this information how you may but don't trust these promoters.

Why Trust The Premier Promoters?

Although it is difficult to comprehend why anyone would want to buy the stocks of worthless scam companies that stock promotion websites recommend to you, especially when we know that the promoters are only interested in helping a third party to sell millions of dollars of worthless stock to their subscribers... It's more difficult to understand why someone would invest long term in one of these companies. The only thing I can say is that over the years certain promoters have proven that their alerts almost always run 25% to 100% and sometimes much more for lower priced stocks under $.10. When these promoters release a pick sometimes tens of thousands of people will rush to buy the stocks that they recommend immediately. This will bring millions of dollars of buying volume into these penny stocks, which will cause a tremendous short-term spike in the price of these stocks. The biggest problem with penny stocks being risky is that they typically have no volume. When I say millions I mean these stocks sometimes become as liquid as a NASDAQ listed stock which trade $20-200 million of volume per day. Since many of these stocks have small floats, the price will usually rise between 20% and 200% in fifteen to forty minutes! The main premier promoters only release stock alerts approximately once a month to once every six weeks, unlike some secondary promoters that release crappy picks every day. They usually send teaser emails at least a few days before each of their picks, to announce the date and time of their upcoming alert although this is not always the case.

Certain promoters may release their picks through a landing page which they provide as a link in their teaser emails. Bestdamnpennystocks.com a former premier promoter used to do this, but now they are no longer successful and it is believed the original owner is now being prosecuted by the FBI. They update this landing page with the ticker on the day and time stated in the first email that they send. Out of their websites, they will usually provide five to seven emails which provide a link to a landing page and the other websites will just send the pick to you through an email. Always use the landing pages since their emails are usually delayed at least ten minutes. What I do is open enough web browsers so that I can open up each landing page in a separate window. I usually zoom out on each window so that I can get about seven windows to fit on two nineteen inch monitors. Right around the market open, I start pressing the refresh button on all of these windows. Most of the time one of the websites will be updated with their alert before the other websites and before the actual release time. Their planned alerts are usually released between 9:33 - 9:40 A.M. EST, so sometimes you will get the alert at 9:30 or 9:31. Getting the pick a minute or two early can allow you to get an execution before everyone else. It's also good monitor an unusual volume and trade count scanner at this time because you can usually determine which stock they will alert by finding the stock with the most volume.

Hard Fills:

In the first few minutes after their alerts are released, it is very difficult to buy the stocks that they pump. In general, all penny stocks are very difficult to buy when they are going up and even more difficult to sell when they are going down. This is due to the fact that the market makers see the buy and sell orders and can, therefore, determine the supply and demand for a stock. For this reason, they know when a stock will move up or down and, therefore, will hold people's orders or raise the bid and the ask rapidly, in order to prevent people from getting filled. These stocks are even harder to buy because there are thousands of people that are also trying to buy the same stock and the market makers do not want everyone knowing that it is possible to make money in the penny stock market. When many orders come in at the same time, the computer algo's that execute orders will not be able to hold a stock down and this usually allows a stock to spike a large amount in a short period of time. If you can jump in on the action during these periods of buy order imbalances and are not greedy, you will make a lot of money in a short period of time with reduced risk, even if you trade large positions such as 100,000-500,000 shares or more

Market Versus Limit Orders:

Even if you use a market order to buy these stocks (which I do not typically recommend), you will hardly ever get filled. In theory, your order should be executed immediately at the current market price, but this almost never occurs. Mainly this is due to the fact that market makers can hold your market order for a certain amount of time before they have to execute the trade and in this period of time when the alert is first released, the stock will increase in price at a rapid rate. Usually, this will cause the current bid price to jump right over the price you are bidding for, which will prevent your order from being executed. Since market orders can be executed at any price, this can potentially cause you to lose a lot of money. For instance, if you put in an order to buy 10000 shares at $1.00 and the stock quickly surged to $1.15 before your order gets executed, but then the buyers disappeared a second later, causing the stock to drop back to $1.00, you would have an immediate unrealized loss of $1500. If the stock continued to rise again above $1.15, which it mostly likely will, your unrealized loss would be eliminated, but this is the risk you face with a market order. I strongly suggest that you only use limit orders to try to buy these stocks, however if you are using a broker like Center Point Securities, then a market may be okay in a worst case scenario situation. In general, I suggest you only use limit orders when trading unless you are trying to buy or short an ultra-liquid stock, which has a $.01 spread and trades billions of dollars of volume.

Do Not Chase!

The #1 rule when trading is never, ever chase a stock past your expected entry price! You either need to receive an execution within 10% to 20% of the price when the alert was released, or you should pass on the trade and wait for a significant pullback and skip the current one altogether. This can be difficult to deal with since many of these alerts run 50 -100% in a very short period of time, but you must stick to this rule or you can potentially lose a lot of money very quickly. The entire increase in the price of a stock is due to these alerts and or a bunch of idiots buying all at once, and nothing more. Once the buyers are done buying, these stocks will crash very quickly most of the time. For this reason, if you do get lucky enough to get executed on your buy order at a good price which is not too far from the initial entry price, you absolutely should not be greedy. You must pick a reasonable target such as a 15% to 50% return and get out fast. You will almost never capture the entire 100% move so do not even try unless you are prepared to fail miserably again and again.

Never over stay your welcome. If your target is 25% above your entry price and all of a sudden the stock spikes up 75%, you should immediately take these windfall profits as fast as you possibly can. This is a gift and you must not be greedy or the profits can slip away in a heartbeat. This is an incredibly important rule to follow, because once one of these stocks starts to drop after the initial run up in the first fifteen to forty minutes, they may never reach the same price again. This is due to the fact that many times these stock are manipulated up from a few cents to $.30 to $1.00 price range prior to the start of the stock promotion. The promoters do this by buying up the entire float or placing large orders to spike the stock. This means they completely control every share of these scam stocks and can do whatever they want. This makes the stock look more attractive to the foolish people that think these are legitimate companies. Most people do not want to purchase a company for $.05 unless they are idiots or degenerate gamblers who think they are going to get rich quickly), but if that stock is suddenly trading at $.60 due to a reverse split or some other form of manipulation such as some large block orders, people may rush in and buy the stock.

Never "Invest" in One of these Scams!

If you are lucky enough to get an execution on one these alerts, you must be very careful and remember that for the most part these stocks are meant for day trading. While certain promotions will run for one to three days, usually your risk will exponentially increase when holding these stocks overnight especially now that the SEC has started halting promotions in as little as a week's time. If you get caught in a stock that is halted you can be sure that the stock will open back up (in a few weeks or even several months later) at 95% discount to the current place, so be careful and trade these in the short term only. If you buy 10,000 shares of one of these stocks at $.50, and it runs to $.75 not long after, you should lock in a profit on 1/2 or 2/3 of the shares you own. You can hold the remaining shares overnight or for two to three days as a lotto ticket, but you will not want to hold them for much longer because these stocks will crash immediately when the stock promoters stop sending out emails. I typically like to sell my remaining 1/3 position overnight on the first day of the alert and then sell into the gap up which occurs 99% of the time, or if the gap is not more than 10%, try to hold the stock a little bit longer and sell some around 10:30 A.M. Occasionally these stocks will even run for 3 days, but stick to the initial 100% rule to be safe since the stocks almost always experience a big pull back or collapse at a 100% gain from the initial alert price. On the remaining part of your position, you should always stop out if the stocks come back to your entry or drops below it on a gap down overnight. Never continue to hold onto a stock like this when it starts to go against you thinking it will reverse. As I mention before these stocks are artificially inflated. When they close red for the day (after being green most of the day, the pump is most likely over and the dump is not far behind. You should be out long before this occurs.

Sometimes these stocks will rise on low volume from for example $.01 to $.80 prior to the start of the stock promotion and then once the promotion is over and the stock crashes, they will fall below the $.80 alert price and come all the way back down to $.01. You absolutely do not want to be caught bag holding one of these companies, so cut your losses quickly and move on. If you were smart and took a profit on part of your position, you will win on the trade regardless of whether you breakeven on the remaining shares. Remember trading profitably is about longevity and protecting your assets not about how much money can you make each time.

How To Get An Execution When Nobody Else Can:

This is another very important part of this guide which very few people know about. A lot of people guard this secret with their lives because it a allows them to earn huge profits. If you have ever seen people posting $20,000 or even $100,000 profits online or on Twitter that they earned due to buying a low priced penny stocks, this is the method they are using to get into these stocks.

The first key to getting executed on your trade is using a direct access broker. Retail brokers like Scottrade, Thinkorswim, TD Ameritrade, Fidelity, Vanguard, Options Express, Tradeking, Questrade, Zecco, Sogotrade, First Trade, Merril Edge, Just2trade, etc. will not allow direct routing and, therefore, they are worthless when buying penny stocks. Some of these won't even allow you to buy Pink Sheet stocks! Please re-read the last two sentence and realize you will most likely lose money or just waste your time if you try to buy penny stocks through a majority of retail brokers. The main reason is because many of these brokers route through one single market maker known as NITE, and if nobody is offering shares for sale through that market maker at the time of your order, it will just sit there and not be executed. On top of this, market makers in the OTCBB and Pink sheet markets do not necessarily have to honor your orders like they must in big board companies listed on the NASDAQ and NYSE exchanges. I believe on the OTCBB they are supposed to execute your orders in a certain period of time (usually under 10 seconds), but this rarely occurs. You can trade these type of stocks through some retail brokers, but if the promoter is selling shares through a non-retail market maker like BMAS, you have no chance to get an execution. In order to get into these stocks, somebody must sell you their shares and mostly likely the only people that may be willing to sell at the beginning of the promotion are the market makers and the promoters.

I use Speedtrader.com for buying these type of penny stocks since it is the best broker for buying OTC penny stocks. I also use Speedtrader for buying and shorting listed penny stocks and higher priced stocks as well. I occasionally will also use Interactive Brokers, another direct access broker, however, they charge $.005 per share for their commissions which can be more expensive when you are buying stocks under $.50 where you need to trade 5,000+ shares. Speedtrader's commissions are $2.95-5.95 per side (about $6-12 per trade) for an unlimited amount of shares, which is a good rate. The more you trade, the lower the rate they will offer you. You may also incur ECN fees in addition to the commission which can be much more if you use an ECN like ARCA OTC, which charges $.004 per share in addition to the fixed commission. Commission are not really a big deal if you take a few trades per day (which I recommend), but if you trade ten or more trades a day, you will definitely need cheaper commissions. Paying $7 or $10 (14-20 round-trip) per trade with crappy retail brokers like Scottrade or Ameritrade is a guaranteed way to lose money.

Speedtrader requires at least $25,000 to open an account and interactive brokers requires at least $10,000. Speedtrader has ECN fees and also charges software fees as well, but there is no way of getting around this and these fees are just a cost of doing business in the market for traders. I suggest a margin account which requires a minimum of $2,000 to open but you can start with a cash account with some brokers. The only issue with interactive brokers is that sometimes the stock alerts by the premier promoters will not be cleared through the DTC, which is a clearing house. When this occurs you will not be able to trade the stock through Interactive Brokers so it is best to have an account with both. In general interactive brokers is not good for buying penny stocks but it can be good for shorting them. It is a very good broker for trading stocks above $5.00 as well since at .005 per share you are only going to have to pay $.50 to trade 100 shares.

Although E*TRADE is not a direct access broker, they do allow routing through the market maker ETMM, which is used by a lot of penny stock traders. For this reason, if you can't afford to open an account with Speedtrader, than E*TRADE is a good alternative. E*TRADE may charge you up to $100 a month to use their software E*TRADE Pro. You cannot substitute E*TRADE Pro for my suggested charting software Quotetracker or Medved Trader because E*TRADE does not have the proper indicators to configure my system correctly.

Finally, Schwab is no longer allowing many direct access brokers to use their route. They execute orders through the market maker UBSS and if you have an account with Schwab, you can route through this market maker. Schwab generally is a pretty crappy broker since it is a retail broker, but it can be useful in certain cases, however for trading non OTC stocks I would not suggest this broker. If you have excess trading capital and four or more 20 inch monitors, it is not a bad idea to have an account at all of these brokers to ensure you have access to all of the routes, but it is certainly not necessary. If you plan to trade large positions in hopes of earning huge profits like $10,000 to $50,000 or more per trade, it is essential to have an account with many of these brokers. Ideally, you'll want to deposit at least $25,000 per broker but this obviously is not realistic for most new traders and it certainly isn't a requirement.

Direct Order Routing:

Speedtrader.com will allow you to route trades through a number of OTC market makers and ECN's. You can do this by clicking on the level 2 quote panel on the actual market maker, under the MMID column or manually selecting market makers from the drop down menu. This is essential when trading these types of stocks because the promoters will route their sell orders through specific brokers and if you cannot place a buy order with that specific route, you have no chance to have your trade be executed. Speedtrader.com also allows to re-route your orders to certain market makers that you cannot route to directly. For instance, you can place a buy order through NITE, with a re-route command to the institutional market maker AABA. This is usually slower than a direct route, but it is better than nothing and occasionally this could allow you to earn a profit, or prevent a huge loss, when you cannot directly route through the standard routes NITE, ARCA, AUTO, ETMM, and UBSS. To re-route an order select a standard market maker such as NITE and then put the MMID for the market maker you want to re-route to, into the box next to the main route selection menu (in this case NITE).

Provided you have enough buying power $25k+ and can day trade an unlimited amount of times in and out of a stock, you'll want to employ many (5-10) limit buy orders when trying to get an execution in these promotions. This is imperative if you want to get into these stocks near the beginning of the promotion when the buying volume is extremely highly when your risk is greatly reduced. This is the hidden secret behind getting an execution when nobody else can, which not many people know about. For instance, if the current market makers/ECN on the ask are NITE at 1.01, UBSS at 1.01, ARCA at 1.02 and AUTO (also known as SBSH) at 1.03, you may want to put in four separate orders to buy the stock at these prices, and select the proper route that coincides with each price (for example 2500 shares through

NITE at $1.01, 2500 through UBSS at $1.01, 2500 at $1.02 through ARCA, and 2500 at 1.03 through SBSH (AUTO). You should also place a bunch of other orders through NITE and ARCA around the current ask price since NITE and ARCA are very common routes that people use to trade these stocks. The size of the spread is important to take into consideration since large spreads can result in immediately unrealized losses. Rest assured, if you are trading off the premier promoters alerts within a few minutes of the initial alert, there is an extremely high probability that the stock will continue to move a lot higher.

These are some of the most common market makers / ECN's that you will see, but others such as CDEL, VERT, VFIN, LAMP, HDSN, CSTI, ASCM, NOBL, SUNR, MBAY, FANC and more could also be making a market in the stock you are interested in trading. If you want to know who these market makers actually are just put their 4 digit number called the MMID (market maker identification), into Google and add market maker to the search.) If for instance two of your orders get executed and you are happy with a 5000 share position, you could quickly cancel the remaining two orders. You might want place a fifth order .001 above the best bid (current highest bid) using NITE. What this will do is if somebody decides to sell at the bid, your order will be the highest price and should, therefore, get executed. For example, if the highest bid is $.99, you would want to put an order at .991 or even .999 through NITE. When a stock is below $1.00, they will allow you to add additional decimal place. The more limit orders you use, the greater the chance that you will get and execution, but be aware of your buying power and do not try to put your entire capital into a stock unless you can afford to lose 50-70% of this amount.

If other market makers such as MICA, BMAS, BMIC, AYME (and several more) are on the bid or the ask, you probably will not be able to directly route to them, even if Speedtrader or another brokers has the route available. Sometimes this occurs and you will have to try to wait for one of the routes I mentioned above to pop. Alternatively, you could also try a NITE re-route to one of these market makers, but as I said earlier, this can take 30 seconds to 1.5 minutes and rarely works unless the price is going to go against your order. The promoters frequently use these routes as their brokers to dump shares, but most retail direct access brokers will not allow you to route to them. The only issues with this multiple order method is that there is always a small chance you will get filled on every order that you place. For this reason, you have to make sure the total order size of all your orders will not add up to a position size you are not comfortable with. The good news is that there will be thousands of people that are dying to buy the stock from you and therefore, if you get filled 100000 shares when you only wanted 50000, you will almost always be able to sell your excess shares instantly to somebody else in the first 2 to 5 minutes after the alert is released.

Please be aware that when you cancel certain orders such as a buy through NITE, it may take 30 to 60 seconds for your order to cancel. This is very annoying and can be an issue if you only have a small amount of trading capital because you may not be able to place another trade until the order cancels. To get around this when buying you should only put orders on the bid with NITE and they will let you cancel immediately. ARCA will always allow you to cancel your orders immediately but unfortunately, this advantage comes at a higher cost of $.004 per share. Also, note that sometimes NITE plays dirty and will hold your order for 30 seconds to 1.5 minutes and then if you decide to cancel, they will execute the order anyway. You might be able to complain to your broker about this, however, I am not sure they will do anything for you. A lot of times the market maker will hold your order when they know the stock is about to go up and then wait to execute your order until the stock is ready to come down. This goes back to my advice from earlier where I mentioned testing a small order to see if it executes or not. Unfortunately, you have only a small time period where you can enter these stocks so you usually have to just accept the risk.

. If you can get in the pre-market by using and ECN like ARCA you have a much better chance of making money on these stock promotions put out by the premier promoters. The key is you only want to enter in the pre-market if you see large blocks hitting the time and sales. OTCBB stocks rarely trade in the pre-market and therefore when a stock has traded $25,000-200,000 of volume (not shares) during time, there is a good chance that one of the premier promoters alerts could move big at the open. I suggest watching these stock from 8:00 A.M. to 9:30 A.M. EST.

Keyboard Shortcuts:

If available, you will also want to setup keyboard short cuts for your brokers execution platform so that you can quickly adjust your order size. You should even setup a specific round lot position size and route to use with your keyboard such as the F1 key for Buy 10,000 through NITEL (NITE limit order) at the current best ask price. You should do this for each F key, so for F2 you could use Buy 10,000 shares through ARCAL, etc. This will allow you to enter several orders in under 5 seconds instead of the 30-60 seconds like most other people will have to do, which is very important to get your order filled quickly. I personally use Speedtrader's DAS Trader Pro Hotkey's to setup my shortcuts. Speedtrader has a manual for their DAS Trader Pro software which will explain how to do this or you can also contact their technical support department if you have questions or want to know how to setup a custom shortcut.

You may also just want to set up a short cut to change the route of the level 2 screen that you have clicked on such as Crtl+N for NITE, Crtl+R for ARCA, Crtl+A for SBSH (AUTO), Ctrl+U for UBSS, Ctrl+H for HDSN, etc. Note that you have to click on the level 2 screen that you are focused on for the route to change. Setting up a shortcut to quickly change the order quantity will also be very useful because sometimes the premier promoters send an alert on a $.03 per stock and other times they send it for a $.25 or $.45 stock. 10,000 shares of a $.03 stock will do nothing for you so you may want to have various quantities programmed to specific shortcuts such as Ctrl+1 = 5,000 shares, Ctrl+2 = 10,000 shares, Ctrl+3 = 25,000 shares, Ctrl+4 = 50,000 shares, Ctrl+5= 100,000 shares, Ctrl+6 = 250,000 shares, Ctrl+7 = 350,000 shares, Ctrl+8 = 500,000 shares, Ctrl+9 = 1,000,000 shares. When you receive the alert, you will quickly have to decide how many shares to buy, and this hot key will let you change the shares quickly. Combining Ctrl+8 with for instance Ctrl+N will let you buy 500,000 shares through NITE, and then you will just have to click the buy button. Just remember you probably need to enter five to ten orders to get filled, so you should plan your order size for each order accordingly to prevent over exposing yourself to a huge position, in the event that every order gets filled.

Level 2 Quotes & Time and Sales:

Level 2 quotes and time and sales are pretty important to intraday trading. Trading without level 2 quotes could be compared to skydiving with no parachute into a pool of piranhas. Level 2 is basically all of the orders that retail and institutional market makers and ECNs submit to the market at various price levels around the current best bid and best ask (known as level 1 quotes). Time and sales (a.k.a the ticker tape) are the actual price and quantity of each trade that is executed in a stock and the time when each occurs. On big board stocks, this no longer represents all the orders that are executed in a stock because many orders are executed off-exchange through what are referred to as dark pools. Both level 2 and time and sales offer information about what is going on behind the scenes in a stock. While they are much less effective now than they were prior to 2002 for big board stocks (NASDAQ, NYSE, and AMEX), they remain effective for OTCBB and Pink sheet stocks and time and sales or reading "tape reading" is effective for stocks of any prices. Although some people will argue that level 2 quotes are inaccurate because market makers do not have to post the full bid or ask size at each price level, they still are useful if you know what to look for and you combine them with the rest of your trading plan. Level 2 takes some time to get used to it and the best way to learn it is to start watching stocks in real time while they are actively being traded with significant amounts of volume (preferably $2 million worth or more).

In general, the first important thing to look for on level 2 are the market makers that are currently making a market in the stock you are watching. As I stated in the previous section, there are retail, institutional market makers and ECNs. NITE (Knight Securities), AUTO (CITIGROUP), UBSS (SCHWAB), and ETMM (E*TRADE Capital Markets) are common retail market makers. When you place a trade through a retail broker such as Scottrade that does not offer direct access order routing and is, therefore, more or less worthless for penny stock trading, your orders will always be routed through NITE (but not the real NITE market maker but rather a version of NITE with worse executions). NITE is good to use at times, however, you need the ability to route your orders through a number of other market makers as well. Institutional market makers like CDEL, VERT, NOBL, VFIN, HDSN, CSTI, ASCM, AABA, MICA, BMAS, BMIC, and AYME, are commonly seen as well. There are many other besides these as well. The last four are usually seen on the bid or the ask of stocks with a current stock promotion, and therefore, you want to keep an eye out for these "key" market makers. Institutional market makers are usually more important to watch than retail market makers because the institutional market makers normally trade much larger size positions for their clients than retail investors or traders.

The second thing that you will want to watch for is whether the key market makers are on the bid, the ask or both sides of the level 2. When you see a number of institutional market makers lined up on the bid or ask, this tells you that they probably have a large order that they are looking to buy or sell, which signifies support (buyer) or resistance (sellers). If they are on both the bid and the ask, they may be trying to capture the spread (buy at the bid and sell at the ask). If these institutional market makers include any of the four key players that I mentioned above on the ask, there is a good chance that they will be dumping shares for the third party shareholder that is paying for the promotion, which may signal that the stock is about to pullback or collapse depending on which stage the pump is in. You also should pay attention to the size of the orders which are posted to level 2, and whether they are on the bid or the ask. This is particularly important when a stock is spiking or panic selling is occurring. Although large orders can be fake or a market participant can cancel an order at anytime, essentially turning level 2 from a strong to a weak, it still can at times be useful.

During times of high volume, the spread will widen or narrow and the number of price levels may increase or decrease very quickly. When a stock is dropping you will usually notice many market makers on the ask either selling or shorting the stock (you do not know which it is since a short sale is essentially just a sell, but if a stock has just cracked a significant support level, you can assume shorts will attack the stock) and few market makers on the bid. This is called a bearish level 2, because the bid is very thin due to a lack of buyers and it does not take many sellers, or shorts, to drop to the next lower price level. The inverse is a bullish level 2 where there are many market makers posting bids. When many buyers line up on the bid, and one or more market makers post a large bid, for instance, 50,000+ shares in a $1.00 stock, you will usually notice the ask starts to thin out quickly. This occurs because buyers become more interested in the stock and sellers quickly cancel or move their sell orders to a higher price level in hopes of a bigger profit. The reason bidders are more interested in buying is because they think big buyers are supporting the stock and very few sellers are preventing a move to the upside. Note retail market makers were recently forced to show the actual order size that they are currently posting, whereas institutional market makers only have to show the minimum size which is usually 500 shares, even when they may be a buyer or seller of many more shares than that. For this reason, what you want to look for is when a number of orders are executed on level 2 while the market makers are on the bid or the ask.

When combining level 2 with time and sales, the important things to look for is whether a majority of the trades are hitting at the bid, ask, in-between, or above or below. Through Speedtrader, a buy at the ask is shown in green on time and sales. A sell at the bid is shown in red and an order in white is usually executed by the market maker inside the spread. Orders above the best bid are also green, but orders below the best bid are shown in pink. When you see orders occurring several cents or more below the bid, the stock is usually experiencing a panic sell-off, and longs are trying exit the stock at any price they can which usually means they are putting in market orders. This is why market orders can be so dangerous because you could literally get an order executed 20% or more below the current price in extreme cases of panic selling.

The size of the trades that are "hitting the tape" are also important. If a stock is rising, and you notice a large block hitting the ask in green, this may signal that smart money is buying because they are expecting a sudden rise in the stock price. Just as charts display patterns which traders can use to make buy and sell decisions, level 2 also displays its own type of patterns. These patterns occur because level 2 quotes are made up of the buy and sell orders that market participants post and the computer algorithms that market makers use while making a market in the stocks that the follow.

The figure below is a screen shot of level 2 quotes which are provided with the Speedtrader DAS Pro software. The first thing you'll notice is that some of the key market makers are highlighted in orange. I set up my software to highlight these because it is easier to see whether they are posting to the bid or the ask. Notice under the SIZE columns all of the market makers are posting a size of 500 (add two zeroes to the 5 get the correct share size), except for UBSS, which is a retail market maker, which is posting a larger block on the offer to sell 39,000 shares. This amounts to $95,550 worth of stock which is a significant amount of a low priced penny stock, which tells you there may be a bearish sentiment in the stock. Also, notice that there are more market makers at 2.48 and 2.49 level, making the ask seem a bit "thicker." This tells you if may be difficult for buyers to push the stock higher, especially since BMAS and WDCO (no longer operating under WDCO but rather BMAK) are on the offer and they could potentially be looking to sell thousands of shares, but until you see more of the key market makers line up on the ask and larger blocks of time and sales, I would not consider this to be very bearish.

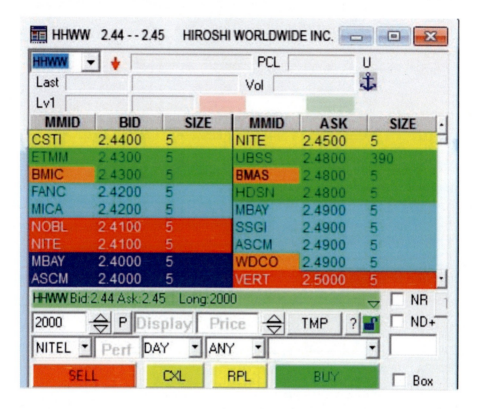

In the next figure below you'll notice that the time and sales has been added. You will want to keep your level 2, and time and sales side-by-side like this. This is an example of a **very bearish level 2**.

Notice all of the market makers lined up on the ask at $2.48 with no other prices showing. This tells you there are many people trying to sell their positions, or short sell the stock on the ask. Also, notice the key market makers on the ask highlighted in orange which tells you that the promotion could be ending, and the dump phase is starting. In addition notice that the electronic computer network (ECN) ARCA, is also a seller. This is the only route that will allow market participants to hide the size of their orders, and for this reason, both large retail traders and stock promoters use this route. (When you have the route ARCAL in the route box next to the little P and to the right of the box where you place your quantity size, you will see a box that says Display. Put a value in this box of for instance 500 shares if you have an order larger than 500, but only want the market to see 500 shares.) For instance ARCA may post a bid of 500 or 50000 shares but somebody could be using it to sell 500,000 shares. You see this a lot of times when lots of orders are hitting the time and sales with ARCA on the bid or the ask, but the stock is not moving. You should also see the large 500,000 block on the ask being posted by ETMM. While this is less likely to occur through a retail market maker like E*TRADE

Capital Markets, it is always possible because some retail traders have large accounts.

Next notice there is a rather large $.08 spread in between the bid and the ask. This occurs when there are a lot of sell orders hitting a stock. I believe the market makers involved in promoted stocks, widen the spread to discourage buyers when they are trying to short the stock, or cause a sell-off so they can accumulate shares for their clients at a lower price. The spread also widens when the market makers feel the risk involved in holding the stock has increased. Next notice the bid is looking very thin because there are not many market makers posting buy orders at consecutive price levels. This means that small sell orders may take out a whole price level and the price will fall to the next posted level which is several cents away. This can be very dangerous if you are long a stock because it can drop very quickly.

Next, look at the time and sale. First notice almost all of the orders hitting the tape are sell orders at the bid. Also, notice somebody just sold 50,000 at $2.37 below the best bid at $2.40. This means they want to exit the stock at any price and it is usually a sign that the stock is going lower. Also, notice that there are many larger sell blocks and very few small buy orders for only a few hundred shares. This tells you that nobody wants to buy this stock since it is experiencing a panic sell-off also know as a bear raid (this is the reason why you must sell into strength in OTCBB and Pink sheet stocks). Finally, notice that the stock has already dropped from $2.56 down to $2.37 in less than 2 minutes. If somebody owns thousands of shares in a pump like this, and the stock is dropping this quickly, they will either be losing all of their profits if they got in early or will be losing all of the money that they put into the pump if they got in late. Sell-offs of more than $.20 in $1.00-3.00

stocks, usually cause major moves to the down side in pumps and may signal the dump is on.

The next figure is an example of a **very bullish level 2**. Once again notice how all of the market makers and ECN are posting a bid of $2.48. Also, notice the same key market makers highlighted in orange, are posting bids at the best bid price. This means many people are eager to buy this stock, and considering the institutional market makers only have to show the minimum quantity, they may be holding orders to buy hundreds of thousands of shares for their clients (you do not know but combining this info with the time and sales, you can see when a large sell order hits the tape, and whether one of these key market makers absorbs it. If they support the stock, there is a good chance it may go much higher. Also, notice the retail market makers ETMM and NITE are positing large 500,000 and 50,000 share buy blocks on the bid. While these could be cancelled at any time, there is a good chance that these large orders will entice of people to buy the stock on the ask, sending the stock higher. Also, notice the institutional market makers MICA, ASCM, and VFIN are on the bid. Considering they only have to show the minimum quantity of 500 shares, there is still a chance that they may be interested in buying many more shares than that for their clients.

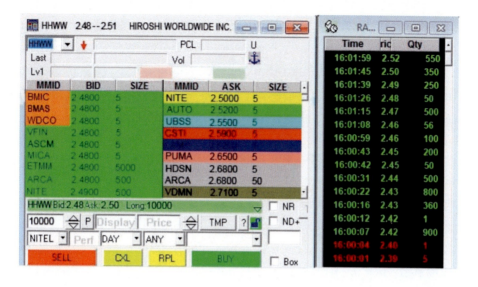

Notice the ask is also looking very thin with only one retail market makers (NITE, AUTO, UBSS) posting sell orders at each price level. Considering the fact that retail traders do not usually trade large positions (except in extremely liquid, promoted penny stocks that trade millions of shares each day), you can assume it would not take many buy orders to take out the current ask and push the stock price up to the next level. Also, notice that none of the key market makers are currently selling shares on the ask. This also means there may not be much resistance since there are no big sellers. The $2.68 area is where more than one market maker and ECN are posting sell orders so you may want to start watching for resistance around this area, especially since ARCA can be a hidden seller. The fact that only one or two buy orders have pushed the stock higher also is a sign that the stock is fairly thin and may make a bigger move.

Moving on to the time and sale, notice that all of the orders are buys at the ask since they are printed in green. Be aware that these are rather large block trades and not retail traders buying 100 or 500 shares. The first buy order for 90,000 at $2.39 has a dollar value of $217,800.

Large blocks potentially mean somebody smart may think the stock is going a lot higher (or somebody could be doing wash trades which essentially trick people into thinking that somebody is very interested in buying the stock. Also, notice there are only two very small sell orders for 100 and 500 shares that occurred a lot lower.

Here are a few other important items I wanted to bring up about level 2. Trades that are way outside of the current best bid and ask prices are called Z trades, for example, a trade $.15 away from the last price of a low priced stock. These trades are posted to the time and sales after they have already been executed and thus are delayed. For the most part, they are irrelevant and should be ignored. The other item that I want to address is erroneous trades. These are usually referred to as bad ticks or a fat finger trade. For instance, if a stock is trading at $2.01 and all of a sudden you see on order hit the tape for 100 shares at $3.12, you can just ignore this. Without a significant news event like a merger or buyout, there is no way a stock can increase 50% in one tick. Alternatively, if you follow the moving averages that I talked about in this guide, you will notice that many times these bad ticks will come very close to touching one of these moving averages. The reason that this occurs is that stocks have a certain market structure which market participants want stocks to follow. For instance, if a penny stock drops $.50 suddenly and blows through a number of key moving averages (which normally act as support), then technically speaking it should come back and test one of these moving averages (which should now act as resistance). Sometimes during panic sells offs a stock moves way too far away from the moving average to come all the way back up to it, so the market makers "paint the tape" to make technical traders think the stock actually did what it is supposed to do. If for example a trader only shorts after a sell-off and subsequent bounce back to the 21 period moving average, then that trader may be reluctant to participate if the typical scenario occurs. Please disregard all erroneous trades that are not close to the best bid and ask.

<u>Target Exit Prices:</u>

Once you enter a trade, you should already have your exit prices planned. It is best to have multiple target prices where in the event that the stock moves in your favor, you lock in 1/4, 1/3 or 1/2 of your position depending on the risk-reward profile of a specific trade and your position size. Once your final target is reached you take your profit, move on and do not look back. Take the ticker symbol off your watch list if you need to forget about the additional profits, you could have made if you were more patient. Understand you will never catch bottoms or tops in stocks consistently and it is better not to. You want consistent, repeatable trades, which will generate profits over the long-term. You are not looking for a home run, but a single or double. If the stock goes up another 200% after you exit, so be it. Just realize that you took predictable profits, stuck to your plan and, therefore, you made the right move. Let the gamblers invest in these stocks for months or years and lose all their money for trying to earn 500% every time.

Major support and resistances levels on the daily chart are a good place to set your targets. You can also use long-term exponential moving averages that may act as resistance such as the 34, 55, or 203 period EMAs. If the pump and dump is a reverse merger stock with a limited trading history due to a ticker change, you will probably want to set fixed targets just prior to the round numbers 25%, 50%, 75% and 100%, 150%, and 200%. You will also need to take into account the risk/reward by calculating the potential upside and downside to the key support and resistance levels (or an Excel spreadsheet). For instance if a stock is trading at $1.00 and has a 2 year support level at $.80, and the next major resistance levels (6 months and 1 year) are at $1.75 (target 1) and $2.05 (target 2), this would provide a very good risk reward of 3.75 and 5.25 times your risk. If the proper stock promoters are sending pump emails on this stock, this will ensure that there is a good chance a stock will have a catalyst to move higher towards your target prices. You will not have very much time to calculate these statistics when an alert is in progress but they are very important so after you enter your orders you should immediately pull up your charts and get to work.

Once in a trade that is going in your favor, you also should employ a mental stop-loss, and if you're up a sizable amount, and the stock starts collapsing on you for whatever reason, you should cut your trade at breakeven. -10% is usually a pretty good stop-loss to use for a low priced stock. In general, I rarely ever expect an alert to run more than 100%. I never try to capture the entire move. Lower-priced stocks in the $.01 - $.10 range have a much greater chance of increasing 100-500% within a short period of time than a stock in the $1.00-5.00 range which normally won't move more than about 100% in a short period of time. Higher priced stocks rarely move more than 20% in a short period of time and this is only due to earnings, a contract, merger, fraud, bankruptcy, etc. which is why you need more money to make money trading higher priced stocks.

For instance one of a former premier promoters past alerts (Note Penny Pic which later was bought out by Awesome Penny Stocks, is no longer in business) on the stock AERN ran from $.01 to $.12 over 6 trading days, unlike $.50-$1.00 stocks which usually only run 25-100% max. During this 6 day period, I received over 350 emails from this stock promoter about this stock which is what helped to push the stock up. The company also released a bogus press release stating they had received a $500 million contract with Exxon Mobil related to gas that they would provide (no joke)! This company is in an exploratory stage and has no cash on its balance sheet, no revenues, and does not earn an income. Why on earth would Exxon Mobile partner up with this micro cap company? Penny Pic was compensated $1.5 million for the promotion and the stock went up 1500% which is a lot more than usual, but $1.5 million is way above average compensation for one of their stock promotions. I only held the stock from $.02 to $.04 for a 100% gain, but you could have held this for multiple days and made a lot more. I chose to take the predictable profits which is usually the smart thing to do because you'll notice the stock dropped 90% off its high in 10 days. See the figure below:

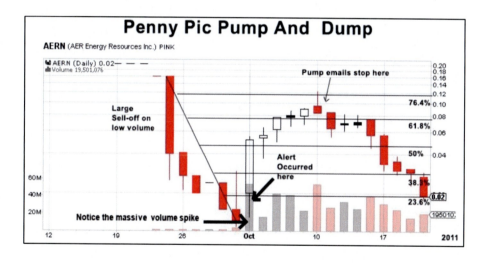

In any case, I have no interest in holding these stocks for more than one day and occasionally overnight on the first day of the alert, but I am becoming more and more reluctant. The longer you hold these scams, the greater the chance that the stock promoter will pull the plug and the stock will quickly drop 50%-70% in minutes! The third party that is paying for the stock promotion will be looking to dump their shares to the unsuspecting suckers while the stock is still rising, so that's why you want to be in and out.

Game Day:

When the premier promoters release an alert, the stocks they promote usually exhibit the same type of intraday chart each time. In the figure below I have drawn this chart from memory and you will need to be able to do the same if you plan to become adept at anticipating exactly what should come next in the sequence of price movements on the first day of one of these premier promoter alerts. Study every individual candlestick of this chart thoroughly and you will have a better understanding of how momentum stocks trade. I referenced momentum stocks and not just the premier promoters pumps on penny stocks because this is what an intraday chart looks like for any high volume stock with significant news, not just penny stocks. The only difference is most real stocks don't move up more than 25 to 50% in one day and that's extreme, whereas these pumps will move up 50 to 100% or more every time. Starting in 2014, there have been many more opportunities in non OTC lower priced biotechs or lower priced tech stocks, (along with other non OTC stocks) and my system works very well for trading all of these stocks.

The alert came out at 9:35 to prevent a big gap in the stock so assuming there are no people front running the pump, the first 5 minutes should have little to no volume as is the case here. When the first email the stock was trading at about $.22 but the market makers were not executing many orders until $.28 which is when the majority of smart people got filled. NITE and ARCA routes allowed to get filled if you put about 5 orders in at various prices including a couple orders on the bid. Other routes were locked up and would not execute until

$.35 which was already 50% above the alert price and, therefore, a bit concerning to be buying in that late. Remember you do not want to chase these alerts. If the stock moves more than about 25% from the initial alert the safest thing to do is ignore it and wait for the midday pullback at the 50-61.8% Fibonacci level to buy into the stock.

The chart below is a 10 minute chart although in general the best way to tell whether the stock will continue to move higher is to watch the emails hit your inbox. Once all of the promoter's websites have released the alert, you can assume everyone has already bought the stock and the stock will not continue to move much higher. Become very familiar with their websites so you can tell which ones you have and have not received. Usually by 10:00 or 10:20 AM EST at the latest you should receive all of their emails. Watch the volume closely because as is the case here when the volume started to drop the rate of price movement started to decline. At a 50% gain, you should be selling part of your position around $.45 to $.48. On top of this in the figure below there was a small pullback around these prices. If the price of the stock was initially below $.50 prior to the alert, these stocks almost always move 75% to 100% or more in the first one to three days. But there are no guarantees in trading and if you get filled a full size of for instance 40000 shares at .28 ($11,200 position), selling 1/3 of your position to lock in $2200 in just a few minutes is not a bad idea. You'll still have 2/3 remaining but you must be a seller when the herd is buying or else when the buying slows down, you will have a very hard time getting executed and may lose big.

As is the case here when the stock has one big push and then its first big red candle, you should be looking to sell another 1/3 of your position into the next failed attempt that the stock makes to break the high. Usually, this will be the high for the day or at least the stock will need a significant pullback of 50% to 61.8% of its range before potentially breaking out and moving higher. For this reason, you are better off locking in another $2200 profit here by selling another 1/3 of your original 40000 share position. Once the support at the $.60 price level is broken, you can be sure the stock will pullback a significant amount over the next few hours. You should be watching the stock closely for a potential price level to buy back the part of your position that you sold, however, you have to be careful not to jump in too early. It often takes two or more hours for the stock to retrace to the 61.8% Fibonacci level where you should be looking to buy and in that time the stock will experience at least two failed bounces. In the figure below the first failed bounce occurred in the $.45 to $.60 price range and the second occurred in the $.35 to $.60 price range. 99.9% of the time after the stock reaches the 61.8% Fibonacci level and bounces it will pullback and retest that level forming a mid-range double bottom time type pattern. The second failed bounce will usually retrace between 61.8% and 78.6% of the range from the high at $.72 down to the low at $.35. Selling will soon hit the stock again and knock it back down in order to scare out the first round of early buyers that bought the first major 61.8% Fibonacci pullback at $.35. Once these people are shaken out, the stock will find support and spike back up again. Buying into the pullback that occurs after this first big green candle at $.41 is usually a good way to get back your full position, assuming a higher lower is formed at the $.40 price level. This usually occurs sometime after 3:00 P.M. EST. As is the case here, after you buy you will want to see the stock start to move back up towards the high at $.70 where you can look to sell 1/3 or 2/3 of your position into the close around 3:55 P.M. EST.

Whether you sell your full position or decide to hold overnight is dependent upon how much the stock moved up from its initial alert price and also whether the stock is closing within $.01 to $.07 of its daily high. If the stock has gained over 100% and has not had a significant pullback of at least 50% to 61.8% of its range, it is usually a better idea to sell your full position. If the stock has gained less than 100% or it has had a sizable midday pullback and then is closing very strong, then you may want to consider holding overnight to sell into the probable gap up that will result from idiots putting in market orders at night while the market is closed. People place these orders because they believe what the promoters say in their second round of pump emails or they missed the initial alert due to their 9 to 5 jobs and want to get in on the action. You never should hold a full position overnight if you have not locked in a sizable profit already and your initial buy price is not a lot lower than the current price. For instance, in the figure below 1/3 of the position was bought at $.28 (the other 2/3 were already sold) and 2/3 at $.41, so the average price is $.36. If you held overnight when the stock closed at $.72 and the stock crashed the following day near the open, worst case scenario you would most likely be able to get out at $.36 (about -50%), which would mean you lose nothing (in fact you would be up $4,400 since you sold part of your position the day before). If you were a late buyer and your average was $.60 and you held overnight and the stock crashed to $.36, you would lose a lot of money. This is why chasing is very foolish.

When you hold overnight and sell into a gap up after the first day of a successful premier promoter alert, it is usually best to sell at 9:30:03 right when the market opens. The reason for this is because this is when foolish people's market on open orders will be executed and you most likely will be able to get out easily since you will be selling to a computer-generated algorithm, rather than a market maker. If the stock has only moved for instance 50% of the alert price then you may be better off selling part of your remaining position into the gap and then holding the rest for a move higher in the stock that will most likely occur between 9:30 and 10:00 A.M. Be careful if you attempt to do this because you must sell while there are still lots of dumb buyers. If the stock gets near the 100% gain price level from the initial alert price, it will drop very quickly with no way for you to get out.

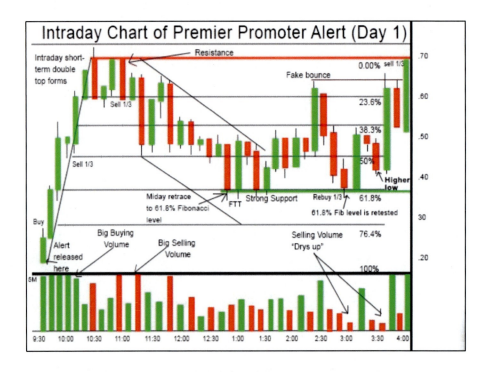

Paper Mailer Pumps:

In addition to stock promoters that use opt-in email pumps to send out their stock alerts, there are also some promoters that will use the US postal mail to send their stock alerts. The most effective stock promoters use a combination of both. Initially, the premier promoters send emails but a few days or a week later they send paper mailers, which cause a persistent rise in the stock way above the initial price released on the first day of the pump. I have explained the way these paper mailers work in another section of this book but I wanted to elaborate on some of the better stock promoters. The following message board forum is an archive of all of the current paper mailer stock promotions that people have received at any given time. **Pump Mailer Forum**. It is a good idea to review this website on a daily basis to see if any new mailers have been posted to it. In recent months, the paper mailers have died down so it may not be active for much longer.

You can also sign up on certain websites to receive their paper mailers directly from the stock promoters. When a stock promotion website asks for your email, name, address, city, state, and zip code, this signifies that they will most likely be sending out paper mailers. If you plan to sign up for a lot of these, it is probably best to sign up for a post office box or a UPS Store mail box for $15 a month. That way your personal mail will not be mixed in with this junk mail but it is up to you. Once you receive a paper mailer or notice a new mailer on the website above, you should automatically look at the daily chart of the stock. Compare the date that you received the mailer to the price action of the stock. Also, check the volume. You should be looking for stocks that are trading $250,000 or more of volume per day and preferably $1 million volume per day. You'll only want to focus on the stocks with a total promotion budget greater than $500,000. If a stock has already gone up multiple days in a row for more than 15% to 20%, it is best to forget about the stock. These stocks may run for a lot longer but they could also crash 50% the second you buy them. It really depends on the third party that is paying for the pump and you really will never know what their goal is except in the case of the premier promoters which have a history of running the same type of promotions.

The stock promoters will send out these paper mailers to different parts of their subscriber list at various times to help manipulate the price of the stock higher. If you are the last group to receive the mailer, you could get hurt badly, so this is why you do not want to chase the stock. You can always wait for a pullback to try to buy the stock, but if the stock promotion is legitimate, the promoter will desperately try to get the stock to close green every single day. Usually, when one of these pumps goes up a lot, the first red day is the beginning of the end for the stock promotion. This is probably the signal that the stock promoter and the third party seller use to determine when they should sell all their stock. This first red day after consecutive green closes is usually when short sellers enter these inflated scam stocks and look to profit from their inevitable 30% - 50% crashes. Usually a $500,000 stock promotion will cause a stock to increase in price for 2 to 5 days before the stock crashes. Larger budgets of $1,000,000 or more have the ability to allow for a stock to increase by several hundred percent and these stock promotions will usually last a few days to 2 weeks but the SEC has started to halt these stocks much quicker so it's very risky to hold these for more than a day or two because you don't want to be caught long a pump and dump when it gets halted.

The way to trade paper mailer stocks is to make sure to get in when the alerts are first released (assuming the stock hasn't moved too much already). Expect to set a first target of about 25% to 50% above your entry. Once your target is reached, sell 1/2 or 2/3 of your position and move your stop-loss to breakeven. On the remaining shares, try to sell part of your position right before any whole numbers like $2.00, $2.50, $3.00, $3.50, etc. If the stock spikes up $.50 to $1.00 per share in a short period of time, after it has gradually been rising $.05 to $.15 per day, either sell your remaining stock immediately or wait for the gap the following morning, and sell at 9:30:05 am EST at the market open. The stock could go higher, however, these large volume days will not last for long and the stock will soon collapse. See the figure below of one of Smallcapfortunes.com most successful stock promotions Hiroshi Worldwide, ticker (HHWW). Unfortunately, Smallcapfortunes.com is no longer a successful promoter like it was several years ago. This company was claiming to be the next True Religion jeans company, whose stock had a run from pennies to $30.00 per share around 2004. True religion sold very over-priced jeans which became trendy and helped them to generate an unexpected profit. True religion started out as a promoted stock but then actually turned out to be a real company. On the other hand, HHWW claimed to sell over-priced T-Shirts for $100 each. Unfortunately, for them, the company was a shell and had no real operations. It never generated any revenue and never generated a profit. It had only a couple of employees and was in an exploratory stage. The stock increased from $1.00 to $3.50 due to a $1.5 million stock promotion campaign and then came crashing down $1.00 per share in one day. You cannot be greedy with these types of stocks. You must be very disciplined and cut your losses quickly if the stock does not do as you expected. Nonetheless, there definitely is money to be made in these stocks.

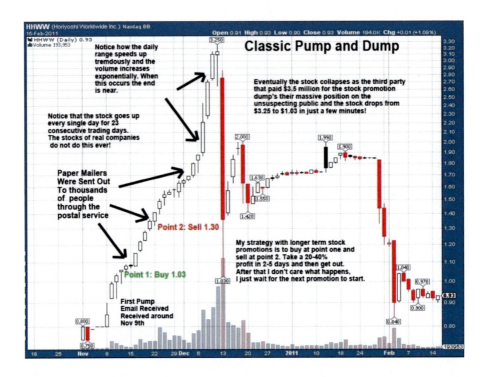

CHAPTER 8:

LONG & SHORT TRADING STRATEGIES

Overextensions & Breakdowns

N aturally when pump and dumps get overextended and the third party decides to liquidate their holdings, eventually they all crash. Many times they drop 50-75% in a short period of time. For this reason, you would think a great way to trade overextended penny stocks would be to short sell them. While this definitely seems logical, there are some so-called barriers to entry and other issues that make this more difficult than you would expect. First of all in order to short sell you must borrow shares. Unfortunately finding low priced OTCBB, Pink sheet stocks, and even lower priced NASDAQ, AMEX or NYSE stocks, is not easy and has become increasingly more difficult as more people try in implement this strategy. Unless you have multiple accounts at some specific brokers known for allowing you to short sell these types of penny stocks, they are difficult to borrow. In order to open accounts with various brokers, you will have to spread your trading capital out. The main brokers have a $25,000 (Sure trader), $10,000 (Interactive Brokers) and $35,000 (Center Point Securities) minimum deposit in order to open an account. You could open an account at just Interactive Brokers but then you could miss out on a lot of opportunities and the profitable opportunities in the penny stock market are usually fairly limited. The other problem is with only $5,000 or $10,000 you cannot day trade since you need at least $25,000 per account to avoid the pattern day trader rule in the U.S. and be able to execute an unlimited amount of trades per day. While you certainly can short these stocks with less than $25,000 ($2000 is the bare minimum for opening a margin account), you put a constraint on yourself if you are undercapitalized and in general constraints are very bad in trading.

On top of these other issues, the shares of these stocks are fairly limited which means if you are not quick to pull the trigger you may miss out. Unfortunately, this means you sometimes have to short a stock early in order to lock up shares but in the process, this could mean you could potentially face unrealized losses as the stock moves higher. Many times a broker will only have shares available in the early stages of a pump and dump. On top of this when you short sell it is not like buying where you can potentially hold for as long as you need to. Since short selling requires borrowing shares, you don't own you must have a margin account. A margin account requires you to put up a certain percentage of equity that you are trying to borrow (typically 50%) and if this percentage drops below a certain level (typically 35%) meaning the stock rises due to a short squeeze, you will get a margin call. A margin call is when the broker tells you to deposit money to increase the equity in your account back to the threshold level or they will cover your short for you at the current market price.

Another issue is something called a buy-in. Since you are borrowing shares of stock in order to sell them, these shares can be called back at any time. For instance, if the original owner of the stock wants to sell their stock, then you might receive a buy-in. 99.9% of the time pump and dumps drop back down at least to where they started but occasionally this takes a lot longer than you would expect. If you receive a buy-in at a bad time like this, you could be forced to take a huge loss. Fortunately, buy-ins usually take at least three days to occur but that is not set in stone.

Shorting an overextension means trying to pick the short term top in a stock that has a very overextended daily or intraday chart. The advantage to this strategy is if you are correct you could earn a large profit very quickly because overextended stocks usually fall quickly. The disadvantage is that picking the top is not easy and if you are wrong you could lose a lot of money even more quickly. Sometimes the stock will pullback a small amount and then push even higher before ultimately putting in the real top, which will trigger your stop-loss. Shorting a breakdown is when you wait for a topping pattern to form (such as a double top) in order to confirm the trend reversal before shorting. The advantage of this strategy is that since you are waiting for a significant support level to crack there is less of a chance that you will be squeezed a great amount quickly. The disadvantage is that the fast money comes when you pick the top correctly but the stock movement on a breakdown is usually a lot more choppy. You can also be squeezed on a breakdown since you are essentially chasing the stock lower after it has already dropped a large amount.

For these reasons it really important to find out where a stock is trading relative to the Linear Regression Channels, Bollinger bands and moving average envelopes, in order to make sure it is extremely overbought when planning an overextension trade and not already too oversold when planning a breakdown trade. Usually, when a stock is trading below the lower Bollinger band and it cracks a support level, it will only drop a little in order to sucker in short sellers and then it will spike. The Bollinger bands and moving average envelopes can also be used for timing an entry on an overextension short sale as well. By waiting for a stock to spike up to the third green or one of the red moving average envelopes, you can be assured that the risk reward is in your favor. Combining this with a measured move, an S4 pivot, a long-term resistance and/or an RSI reading above 93, can make for a high probability setup. If you are interested in learning more about short selling low price stocks, I suggest starting to look to identify the pattern below. Short selling penny stocks is a legitimate strategy if you are properly capitalized, it's just not that easy.

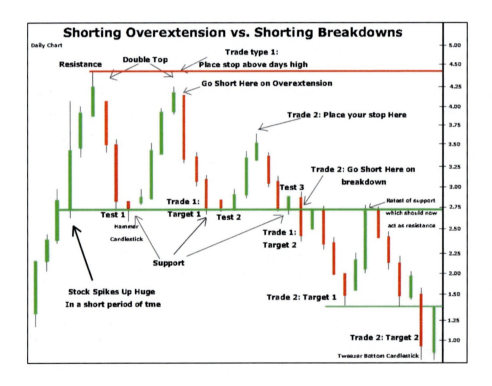

Bounce Plays:

Bounce plays are a type of high risk, high reward strategy where you buy a stock that has just dropped 10-50% or more in a short period of time after a substantial, multi-day or multi-week rally. In general you should only focus on the ultra high volume stocks (which are fairly rare) that have increased by at least 50%+ over the last few days or in certain circumstances a month, due to a large budget stock promotion of at least $500,000 or some other important news catalyst. Bounce plays are also very common in Nasdaq CM, AMEX, and NYSE stocks priced under $25.00, but you certainly should look for higher price stocks which missed earnings, or experience some other negative catalyst and dropped 10-20%, for bounce trades as well. Sometimes people call this strategy "catching a falling knife," and this is justly so because you can potentially lose a lot of money very quickly if you miss time the trade or size your position incorrectly.

Your position size needs to be commensurate with the amount of risk that you are willing to accept in the event that the trade does not work out, plus a small buffer amount due to slippage. When I refer to high volume I mean the stock needs to be trading millions of shares per day, and the number of trades in the stock the day of the crash should be high (typically above 1000). The first reason why this strategy works is because there are a lot of other people whom follow this strategy and they are all waiting for the right time to "buy the bounce," however only a select few traders make big money. The second reason is that any time a stock drops 50% in a very short period of time there will be many short sellers involved in the stock and they will want to take their profits at the first sign of a reversal in the stock. For this reason, their short covering will cause a short-term spike in the stock, which will add to the buying pressure. One thing you have to be aware of is that stocks that drop 50% rarely if ever continue back up to new highs above the price that they traded at before they crashed. For this reason these bounce trades are almost always very short-term day trades of a few minutes to a couple hours. Occasionally it may be okay to hold the stock overnight, however you typically need one or more additional down days after the day that the stock drops 50% to turn the risk-reward profile back in your favor. In either case your risk will increase exponentially when holding your position overnight so your position size is extremely important.

In addition to a stock dropping 50% or more in a short period of time you also need some other indicators to align in order to trigger a potential bounce trade. First you should pull up a daily chart of the stock and draw a Fibonacci retracement from the first day that the pump started (when you received the first pump emails or paper mailer, or the first day a news story was released), to the highest high that was reached during the pump. You could also draw a retracement from the top of the first candle which put in the highest high prior to the huge sell off, down to the current price where you are expected a bounce. If the volume was very low at the beginning, then adjust the Fibonacci retracement to the price where you first noticed decent size volume bars. If the stock was trading 20,000 shares per day this is irrelevant. If the stock had already been trading up prior to the start of the stock promotion, then you should also draw a second Fibonacci retracement line at the actual lowest low.

When pumps eventually crash, they typically retrace 61.8% or 78.6% of the amount that they increased during their move up, before they really bounce. Sometimes a stock will bounce at the 38.3% or 50% Fibonacci retracement levels but these are usually failed bounce attempts. Usually if you draw more than one retracement you will see that the levels overlap. This is called confluence and it is very important to look for price levels where there is confluence. You should also look for major support and resistance levels on the 60 minute or daily charts that line up with these Fibonacci retracement levels, as well as pivot points on the daily chart that coincide with the same prices levels. The S4 support is the most notable one to watch. Sometimes these Fibonacci levels will work well and other times price will fall right through them. Also look at a 60 minute and daily chart with Bollinger bands and moving average envelopes. Note how far the stock is above the upper band. When pump and dumps crash they normally fall at least back to the upper band on a daily chart before bouncing temporarily. On a 60 minute chart the stock will normally drop all the way below the lower Bollinger band before bouncing. If a stock is extremely overextended and has been moving up for several weeks with almost no pullbacks you will probably see the stock drop a lot further than you would expect and it may get all the way down to the 32 period, 3 standard deviation Bollinger band before bouncing intraday. See the figure below on the daily chart with Bollinger bands and moving average envelopes.

99% of the time the stock will put in at least one fake bounce prior to the real bounce and sometimes several. This is what you have to be very careful with because occasionally the stock will bounce a small amount at the 61.8% retracement level, then quickly the bounce will fail and the stock will fall to the 76.4% level where the real bounce occurs. If the difference between the two price levels is large you may experience a large drawdown or the stock may never even bounce back to your entry price. Because these are low priced stocks a small amount of money such as $4000 may buy you 10,000 shares, which would mean every cent the stock moves will be a $100 gain or loss for you. When a pump and dump crashes they sometimes move $.25 to $1.50 in a short period of time so the gain or losses can add up very quickly. As I mentioned earlier if it is easy to buy an OTCBB or Pink Sheet stock during these specific time periods, you are most likely wrong and you should try to exit immediately. For this reason it is best to try a small test position of 100 to 500 shares depending on the price of the stock to see if the market makers execute your trade. If for instance the trade is not executed quickly then you know the stock is going to move higher and you can enter a buy order above the best ask for your full size position and hope to get an execution.

The most important tool for timing a bounce trade in an OTC stock is understanding how to read level 2 quotes and time and sales (which I already covered). Every time a stock crashes level 2 will exhibit a certain pattern. If you learn the pattern you will have a strong chance of timing these bounce trades. If you ignore the pattern you will lose a lot of money very quickly. Once you have a basic idea of what to look for, the best way to ingrain this pattern in your mind is to watch level 2 quotes during the crash phase of as many pump and dumps as possible, and also watch level to for any NasdaqCM, AMEX and NYSE stocks which have sold off more than 10% quickly. It will take some time to get used to the pattern but you will eventually know what to look for. In general when a penny stock starts crashing you will see many large block trades hitting the bid (red prints on time and sales), along with many orders below the best bid, and very few buy orders at the ask (green prints on time and sales).

The spread between the best bid and best ask may widen by a large amount. The reason that this occurs is because people are panic selling, and want to exit the stock as fast as possible, and short sellers are "whacking" any bidders that step up to buy). Under these circumstances market participants, including market makers trading under the MMIDs such as BMAK, BMIC, BMAS, VERT, MICA and more will lower their bids and sometimes block the best bid. Since most people cannot route orders to these market makers, they will have to route to a retail market maker or ECN like AUTO, UBSS, NITE, ETMM, or ARCA which could be as much as $.10 or more below the best bid. This will cause a stock to fall very quickly. You will also notice that the market makers will line up on the ASK causing it to look very "thick", with many market makers trying to sell large positions at every price level. On the other hand the BID will start to look very "thin" with very few market makers at each price level, and some gaps in between price levels. Pay attention to the location of market makers like BMAK, BMIC, BMAS, and VERT on the bid. Sometimes the stock may be trading at $1.00 after it dropped from $1.60, but BMAK will be positioned at $.70 which probably means the stock is going to continue to keep dropping. Also pay intention to the size that these same market makers are choosing to show. When they want to stop a stock from plummeting they may sometimes post a large 500,000 or even 5,000,000 share buy orders on the bid. Sometimes these orders are just used to manipulate the stock in order to con bounce players into immaturely buying, and will be quickly cancelled, and other times they may be a real buy order which may trigger a bounce in a stock that just crashed.

When large buy orders pop up on the bid at the same time that the stock reaches the 61.8% Fibonacci level, there is a good chance that the stock promoters are interested in supporting the stock at the current price. If these large block orders never show up then you must look for the ask getting thinner (sellers disappearing or raising their bids) and the bid getting thicker (buyers placing new orders and the bid price increasing as people raise their prices that they are willing to buy the stock at.) Combine this with the prints on time and sales going from mostly red prints which are sell orders at the bid to more green and white prints which buy orders at the ask or last price traded and the bounce most likely will occur. As I said before you almost always want to see one failed bounce attempt prior to entering the stock. Although this is not always the case most of the time a stock will experience an intraday double bottom (VV) pattern, rather than a (V) bottom.

The hardest part is trying to get an execution because if you wait for all of the sellers to "dry up" the market makers will not want to fill your buy order. In order to get filled you need to be placing a buy order at the time when the first round of bounce players are getting stopped out as the stock takes out the low. To do this you want to place an order on the bid, rather than on the ask and some somebody will most likely hit the bid with a sell order which will execute your buy order. All of the other indicators also need to line up at the same time, or else you could lose a lot of money very quickly. This really is the only way to get an execution in these types of stocks when they crash. Otherwise the market makers may only be willing to execute your order $.10 or even $.25 above the price where the stock bottomed, and then the stock will immediately pullback causing a drawdown or even worse a failed bounce attempt which will scare you out of the stock. When you enter a stock after the first bounce attempt has failed, there is less of a chance that the stock will fall back down and immediately take out the low again. It may however pullback 50%, 61.8% or 78.6% of the amount that it initially bounces before continuing higher. For this reason you will want to place a hard stop or use a mental stop below the intraday low and then trail your stop up to just below the 61.8% retracement level after the stock bounces, retraces 61.8%, and then moves higher.

If you time a bounce correctly, there is really only one place that the stock should go, and that is up. For the most part the stock should rapidly increase in price very quickly. In these situations stocks need to bounce quickly or else there is a good chance that the promoters are selling into the bounce buyers and the bounce will soon fail when the buyers are done entering the stock. If you buy into a stock that just crashed from $2.50 all the way down to $1.10 in one hour without much of a pullback of any kind, when the bounce finally occurs, it should quickly move up at least $.15 to $.20 almost instantly after you buy into the stock. This move "on air" or low volume, occurs because everyone wants to buy into the stock all at the same time and market makers will quickly raise their offers when they see the huge amount of buy orders hitting the ask. If you try to enter when the herd is entering it will usually be too late and the market maker will not execute your order.

You should try to exit your trades at three predetermined prices targets in 1/3, or else sell 1/4 of your position at each of the first three targets and then hold the remaining 1/4 using a trailing stop. The first target I like to use is at or around the 8 period exponential moving on a 5 minute chart. This is a very conservative target that will almost always be reached quickly when a stock crashes, reverses, and then bounces. The second target is either the 13 or 21 period exponential moving average on a 5 minute chart. In an extremely weak stock, this sometimes acts as a strong resistance level when the bounce fails. At other times, the stock will pullback at this price level, but quickly find some support and break the short-term high moving towards the next target. The third target is the 34 or 55 period exponential moving average, the VWAP (found in most charting software), or the 50% retracement from the previous swing high where the sell off started or the last fake bounce occurred. Sometimes these will all cluster together and other times they will be further apart so you can have some discretion. The final target is at the 55 period exponential moving average on a 5 minute chart or the 61.8% retracement level, but you will want to tighten your stop up to the 50% retracement level drawn from the swing low where the stock bottomed up to the highest price that the stock has bounced back to.

As the stock moves to the next retracement level, you will want to trail your stop loss up to the next higher retracement level. Eventually, your target should be reached or you should be stopped out. After a stock crashes, bounces 50% or 61.8% and then hits resistance and turns back down, it will be very difficult if not impossible for you to get out at the price level that you intended to. This is the reason why I sell a portion of my position at each of these price levels because it ensures that I lock in a profit, and it prevents me from getting greedy and losing all of my profits, or worse yet, taking a big loss. When an OTCBB or Pink Sheet stock is rising, you can either sell at the bid or at the ask. They will usually execute your order instantly and you will know the stock is going to continue moving higher. If you try to sell your first quarter or 1/3 of your position at the first target and your order just sits there without being execute for more than 1 minute, you should seriously consider cancelling the order and placing a new order at or below the ask to attempt to exit the stock immediately. As I mentioned earlier, if you have a hard time selling the stock, there is a very high chance that the stock will move a lot lower very soon.

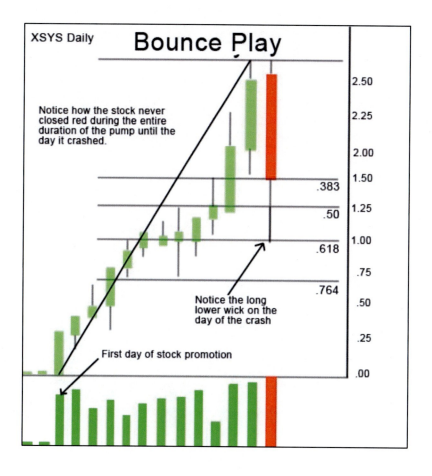

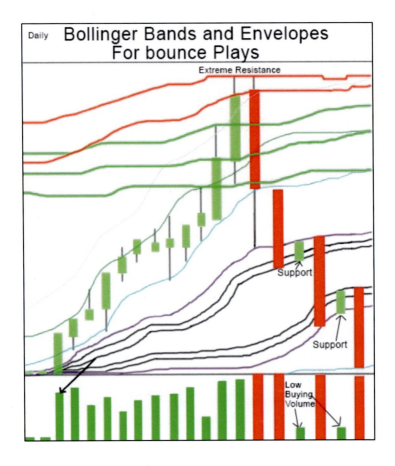

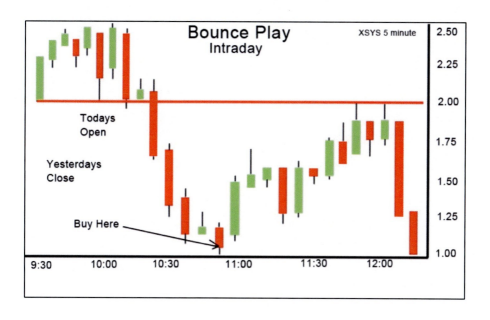

CHAPTER 9

EXPLANATION OF MY DAILY ROUTINE

To consistently make money in the market you need to have a plan that you follow day in and day out. While trades will not come your way every day, you have to be patient and realize that you should only be interested in the high probability setups which in this case are the alerts sent out by the premier promoters and trade setups which fit some of the patterns in this book. If you stick to the stocks that the premier promoters alert and the long-term snail mail pumps, you should make money. It is not too hard to make money in the market, but it is hard to keep it if you deviate from the plan.

Every night after the close I check percent gainers on OTCBB and Pink sheet stocks using the scanning feature built into Medved Trader software. I also scan for unusual volume on stockfetcher.com, which costs $8.95 per month. I am particularly interested in low priced stocks that have moved up a lot or stocks which have not moved up much, but have had a significant increase in volume over their average daily volume. I will also scan for NASDAQ, AMEX, and NYSE stocks with a percentage gain greater than 8% since these stocks are typically the ones with the highest volume and greatest range. Around 9 pm I check my Gmail pump email account and look for emails from the premier promoters. If I am in a stock overnight, I will check for secondary promoters that are releasing pump emails on the same stock that I am holding. I also check the paper mailer message board which I provided in the last chapter to see if there are any new long-term, high compensation pumps. If I find a potential pump, I can quickly identify whether a stock is being promoted through emails by typing the ticker symbol in my Gmail search box. This will search my whole inbox for emails which have this ticker symbol.

I also check the following link to see which stocks are on people's radars. While almost all message boards are full of morons and fools that believe in these scams and are therefore worthless, there is one board on InvestorsHub.com, which I find very useful but 99.9% of other message boards on Investors Hub are completely worthless and I suggest you NEVER trust anything you read on message boards. The old owner of InvestorsHub.com was actually a convicted felon stock promoter so be warned if you already frequent this site! I mean it if you are one of these people who goes on to message boards looking for other people's opinions on stocks this needs to end right now. The board is called Live Day Trading and some of the world's best penny stock traders post messages on this board so I suggest checking it quite frequently to see which stocks people are talking about. Scroll down on the page until you see the messages posted by members. Pay attention to the messages from the moderators and ignore most of the others. You will notice that any stock that has volume and momentum at any given time will be posted to this board. Do not buy a stock just because somebody on this board says it is a good buy. Only use the board for finding new stocks and then type the ticker into my trading system and find out where the stock is trading in the spectrum of prices and see if an opportunity presents its self on the daily or intraday charts. Also, do your research to find out which promoters are pumping the stock (if any) by checking your pump email account.

Stock Scanning:

I use equityfeed.com to scan for stocks during the trading day in real time. It cost about $100 a month for stocks under $5.00 per share or $160.00 a month for stocks of any price. Even though this is not cheap, it is well worth the cost if you plan to day trade more actively because it tells you all of the stocks that are currently moving and is highly customizable for basically any type of scan you can imagine. If you plan to take trading serious, you must have an intraday scanner, and you will have to pay for it. If a stock is on one of my scans, it means it meets certain minimum criteriawhich helps to increase the chance that other traders are watching the stock and will look to take the same trades as me. Fortunately, this software is not needed to trade the alerts which are sent out by the premier promoters, but it can sometimes help to identify some of these stocks prior to the start of the stock promotions which can be very profitable. To do this you need to set up a premarket scan that searches for stocks that have low average volume, but large volume blocks currently hitting the tape (greater than 50,000 or 100,000 shares). The price range should be $.03 to $5.00 and the volume should be set to 100,000 shares to filter out illiquid stocks. You also want to set the number of trades to 25 or 50.

Equityfeed.com also allows you to setup custom filters based off of various technical criteria, which will constantly show you which stocks are moving during the trading day. The software provides a market view, index view, sector view, short interest view, market internals and more. There is also a place where you can build your own scan for filtering out criteria's such as: $ volume, # of trades, average daily volume, stocks making new highs/lows, stocks that have retraced or bounced a specific % off their day high/lows and a whole lot more. I utilize all of the parameters I just listed and change the price range, volume and exchange to create various scans. The software also has real-time news which allows you to search for specific keywords and filter out news on specific stocks listed on the OTCBB and Pink sheets exchanges. It includes intraday charting, level 1 and 2 quotes ($20.00 per month extra), time and sales, watch lists, alerts and more. It is very easy to learn to use this software and their technical support is very good.

As a backup, I also use Interactive Brokers TWS software to scan for stocks. The only downside to this is that there are a lot less scanning parameters to choose from when compared to Equityfeed, but TWS only costs $10.00 a month if you have an account with Interactive Brokers, and is free if you trade enough. I have 5 scans which I constantly keep running on one of my monitors. To setup, a scan go to the Trading Tools menu and choose **Mkt Scanner**. You can right click on the heading "Stock Scanner" and then choose to detach so that you can place the scan anywhere on your monitor. The first scan I use is the "Top Trade Count" scan for OTCBB and Pinksheet stock (make sure to click the boxes for only these two exchanges). This scanner shows me penny stocks which have the most number of trades. Considering most penny stocks are very illiquid and sometimes all of the volume can come from a couple large block trades, it is important to watch this scan. I typically look for stocks trading 500+ trades per day, although when an alert is first released this number will be usually lower. The second one I use is the "Most Active" scan for OTCBB and Pinksheet stocks. It shows all of the stocks with the highest volume and the biggest percentage gainers or losers. To sort for the biggest percentage losers or the highest volume stocks, you just click on the **Chg %** or

Volume columns. Since lots of traders are interested in the highest volatility stocks, each day this is an important scan to follow. The third one I use is the "Top Volume Rate " scan for OTCBB and Pinksheet stocks, which shows the stocks with the greatest volume spikes at any given minute. This scan sometimes helps to find newly promoted stocks right when they are released or even pre-promotions before they begin. The other two scans I use are the "Top % Gainers" and "Top % Losers scans" for NASDAQ, AMEX, and NYSE stocks. I use these to find listed stocks which have spiked or dropped a large amount. Once I have these stocks I can plug them into my trading system and in particular, my Buy/Sell Zones to find overextensions to short sell, or stocks that have dropped way too much for bounce plays. See the figures below for the settings for these scans.

Lastly, I use the high of day/low of day scanner on Speedtrader's Das Pro software. I set the price range from $.20 to $50 and the volume to 500,000 shares. I also set the average volume to 350,000 shares and the Price % Chg to greater than or equal to 5%. This scan is useful because stocks that make new highs or new lows flash green or red and this brings a lot of attention to these stocks.

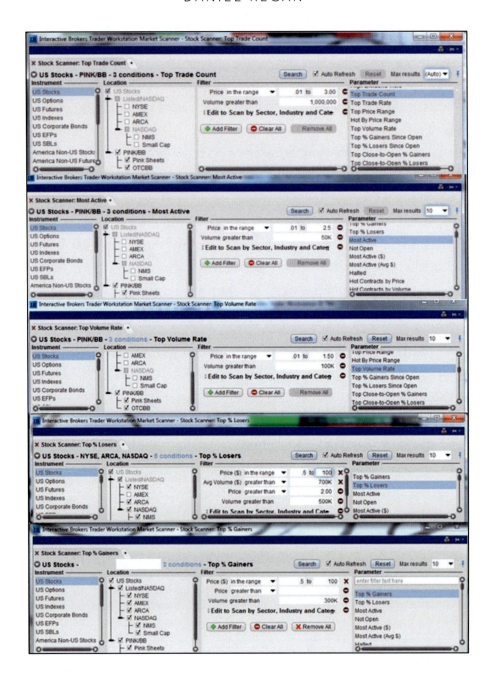

The figure below shows what the scans output.

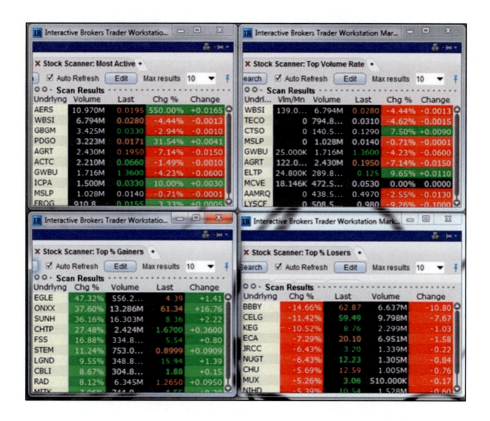

Any stocks that I find interesting, I will place on my watch list in Quotetracker and Medved Trader. Then I will pull up a daily, 60 minute and 5 minute chart for each of these stocks and draw in important support and resistance levels and trend lines/channels. I will also make sure my Quotetracker is configured to add the exponential moving averages that I listed above onto all of my charts both intraday and historic. I will review the stocks that are currently in play (also known as trading on high volume due to current stock promotions just in case I find an opportunity to re-enter a stock on a panic sell-off using my Buy/Sell Zones). Once I have my list, I will place each stock in a separate 5 minute chart.

<u>My Personal Trading Setup:</u>

I trade with five 19" Acer monitors attached to a desktop PC computer, with an ATI quad monitor PCI-E graphics card and one Tritron See2Extreme USB 2.0 graphics adapter. You do not really need more than two monitors to trade my method but it does make life a lot easier. Since trading is a business and businesses require capital to get started, it makes sense to invest money in your trading setup. A quadruple monitor video cards cost about $200 on eBay which is not cheap (although I found mine used on there for $128), however I found that I could never get two dual monitor cards to work correctly together, even under Windows 7, which is supposed to support them and would have been a lot cheaper.

I custom built my computer myself although any fast computer with a lot of RAM and at least a dual video card, should do. My computer is has a quad core processor with 16gb of memory and it runs all of my trading software smoothly. On the first monitor, I have 16 charts displayed through both Medved trader (On the second monitor, I place my TWS Interactive Brokers watch list and the TWS scanner. On the third monitor, I place my Speedtrader DAS Pro order entry software which includes my level 2 quotes, along with a scrolling high/low ticker list for finding the most active stocks. On the fourth monitor, I place the Equityfeed.com software for intraday scanning and real-time news. On the last monitor I have a few charts set up (1 minute with EMA's, 5 with EMA's, 15 with Volume by Price, 60 buy/sell zones, 240 minute linear regression channel, 390 minute linear regression channel) to monitor a stock which I am currently trading and I also use this monitor for web browsing. These multi-time frame charts are setup to display my trading system which includes the Buy/Sell Zones, pivot points and exponential moving averages, and allows me to draw in Fibonacci retracements, Fibonacci extensions, and measured moves.

Becoming a Self-Sufficient Trader

Some words of advice: If you want to make money in the stock markets then you will need to learn to be a self-sufficient trader. There are thousands of so-called gurus out there that are offering trading alerts through emails, text messages, IMs, online chat rooms and other ways. Some of these people charge a few hundred and others charge a lot more. A few of them are legitimate and actually earn real profits, but 99% are just con artists that are trying to take your money and provide you little if any tradable alerts. They operate these services because they are not good at trading and, therefore, use the excuse that they are teachers in order to earn a living from the trading industry without actually trading. Over the last 14 years, I have learned it is just not possible to try to follow somebody else's trades and think that you will be able to consistently earn a profit. Trading requires market timing and alerts are always delayed. Even "liquid" penny stocks are too illiquid and move too quickly to get the same price as the guru. On top of this, you'll never be able to follow alerts 100% flawlessly unless you know the guru's strategy inside and out, and that's almost impossible since 95% of traders lose. Furthermore, if you have to follow somebody else's trades, you are most likely are not a good trader yourself and, therefore, will fall into this category.

For instance, if a guru has 1000 paying subscribers, each with $10,000 in their accounts, this will theoretically bring as much as $1,000,000 in buying volume into a stock each time the guru sends out an alert. Most penny stocks have both a low market cap and low outstanding shares and, therefore, it does not take many buyers to move the price of them. When you try to follow someone like this, you will almost never be able to get the same price as them. If they typically earn $.20 per share, per trade, you can expect to earn half this amount. This is okay on the winning trades, but the real problem arises on the losing one's since profitable trading comes down to managing your risk. When a trade goes against the guru, assuming they are a good trader, they will take a loss quickly. Unfortunately by the time subscribers receive their sell alerts, the stock will most likely have moved way below the guru's exit price. On top of this, there will be 1000 other people that will be looking to sell the stock at the same time. This will cause the stock to drop very quickly and will magnify the size of your loss exponentially, each time a losing trade occurs. The guru probably will get out of all of their trades breakeven or at a small loss and their winning trades will offset their losers, resulting in a net profit (if they use proper money management). Unfortunately, your losses will be so much larger that you will either breakeven or incur a net loss. In my early days of trading, I experienced this situation numerous times and I just wanted to warn my readers that following somebody else's trades is a sucker's game, and will almost never result in consistent profit over the long-term regardless of what anyone tells you. If you want to make money in the market consistently, the only way to do it is to learn a profitable strategy yourself. Start with my strategy and trading system and customize it as you see fit to suit your personality or you won't be successful.

The Road To Consistent Profitability

What is needed to become a consistently profitable trader? This is a question that many people ask, but never receive a clear answer to. The first reason for this is because most people are not consistently profitable yet claim to be and, therefore, do not have an answer. The second reason is because the answer is really dependent on each individual person. There are four main stages in the journey to consistent profits. **1.** The losing trader. **2.** Breakeven trader. **3.** Marginally profitable trader. **4.** Consistently profitable trader. Every trader that remains in the business long enough will experience these stages regardless if they want to or not. Assuming a person utilizes my method, it still will probably take the average person 1-2 years to become consistently profitable. You may make money immediately, but only if you follow everything I have taught you 100% perfectly from the beginning and that will not be easy for most people. In fact many will never even come close. Being consistently profitable is not just dependent on having a profitable trading strategy which gives you positive expectancy because this is just one piece of the puzzle. There is a lot more required.

For a strategy to work for you, you first need to learn it inside and out. You essentially need to be 100% confident in the trading methodology that you use and make sure you can internalize the method. After you utilize my strategy over and over again and experience both losing and winning trades, one day everything will just click. You will start to feel like you have become an expert at trading my method. A good example that I like to give is how the main character Neo from The Matrix feels lost throughout the whole move and then at the end he realizes that he is "The One," and suddenly he starts to take on super human powers. When you internalize my strategy correctly, you will feel as though you almost cannot lose. Of course you will have small losses from time to time, but for the most part, if you stick to your plan 100% and cut your losing trades quickly, you will make money over and over again.

Some people may be uncomfortable trading volatile penny stocks. Some people may not like watching every tick that a stock makes and instead just want to hold long-term investments. For these people, my own strategy may not be suitable but you can tailor the system to fit your personality by using only daily or week charts, and instead swing or position trading. Your personality plays a large role in whether or not a particular trading strategy is suitable for you and you will only find this out by testing it in the real world. The only way you will be able to achieve this is by experiencing the trading setups first hand until you know what "should occur" and how to adapt when it does not.

In addition to this, you will also need a proper broker, the capability to trade in and out of a stock, adequate trading capital, the proper trading software with real-time charting (Medved Trader or Esignal is the trading software that I highly suggest you use) and level 2 quotes (Medved Trader provide free level 2 quotes with a TD Ameritrade account or else Speedtrader and Interactive Brokers will also provide this for a fee). Having your charts setup correctly with the suggested indicators, and the ability to compute the proper position size and risk exposure as a percentage of your trading capital on the fly is also imperative. You'll also need to know how to calculate your entries, exits, and stop-losses and have the discipline and focus on sticking to them. In addition, you will have to be at the computer or have mobile trading access on your smartphone at the correct times when potential trade alerts may occur and have the discipline to stay out of the market when there are no ideal setups. This is very important since trading at the wrong time of day will greatly reduce your chance of success. All of this is what constitutes your trading plan and without every one of these components, I can assure you that you will never earn consistent profits. This is the reason why almost everyone fails at trading because they do not realize how important all of these factors really are. Do yourself a favor and make sure you can cover each of these factors or else save your money.

<u>Final thoughts</u>

Even with all of the information that I have provided, trading will be challenging. It requires dedication and focus, but unfortunately, most people do not realize this. In theory, it should be fairly easy to trade successfully, but, in the beginning, emotions such as fear and greed will most certainly cloud your judgment and cause you to make poor decisions. If you read this guide inside out several times (this is a requirement, not a suggestion) and follow the directions that I have provided, there is no reason why you should not make a lot of money in the market. I have provided a detailed overview of how I trade successfully day in and day out.

It is now up to you to see if you have what it takes to do the same. If you deviate from the plan or try to follow only part of it (such as using a retail broker like Scottrade, instead of one of the suggested brokers, or trying to trade with only $300), unfortunately, it is very likely that you will lose all your money. I have tried my best to provide an easy to follow guide. Before you decide to place a live trade, you should definitely watch the market for at least a few months and get a feel for how stocks trade. As I said before, penny stocks are very volatile and risky, but you can help to minimize this risk by following the rules and directions that I have provided in this E-book.

I worked hard on writing this guide and I appreciate any feedback that my readers have for me. Please send me reviews of my course to **Email Me** or support@beatstockpromoters.com. In return, I will provide you a **special bonus** which you will find very beneficial so don't miss out!

The Next Step?

If you feel like I have provided you good value, and are looking to take your trading to the next level, you may want to consider my second course and E-book **Penny Stocks Behind The Scenes 2: Advanced Strategies For Becoming A Better Trader**.

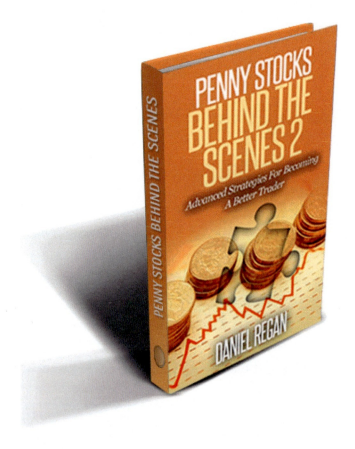

I spent the last 2 years creating this second course and E-book and many people have told me it's even better than my first. Penny Stocks

Behind The Scenes 2 delves much deeper into the indicators that make up my trading system and how they are all inter-related. It is focused more on small-caps penny stocks and less on OTC's, but will show how you can use my system to trade any type of asset, not just stocks. It is 370 pages long, so it has much more information than this E-book.

Most notably, it includes examples of 30 of my real trades with a detailed explanation and hundreds of annotated charts explaining my thought process for placing each trade. I believe these trade examples are the key to learning to apply the patterns in my first E-book to the market in real time. You certainly can decide for yourself if you think you are ready to begin live trading, or whether you feel like you want to educate yourself more thoroughly and gain more confidence first.

The other great benefit of my new E-book is that it includes a whole chapter on creating your own written trading plan from start to finish. This is very important and I believe it will be extremely useful. It also has a chapter with detailed instructions on configuring my trading system in Medved Trader the exact same way that I use the software.

This is very important and I believe it will be extremely useful. The purpose of this new E-book is to help people to gain their financial freedom and if they so choose, become full-time professional traders. Even if this isn't your goal, and you just prefer to keep your day job, this new E-book will still be very helpful because it will tie everything together and really streamline the whole trading process. I believe investing a bit more time and a little more money in educating yourself, will increase your chances of making big money in the market, but don't take my word.

Whats Included:

- ✔ *Detailed 370 Page Ebook (Ipad, Kindle, Android, Etc)*
- ✔ *My Personal Watchlist For Following The Stock Market*
- ✔ *A Trading Journal For Tracking Your Progress*
- ✔ *My Personal Reading List Of The Best Trading Books*
- ✔ *List: Answers To Many Important Trading Questions*
- ✔ *Guide: How I Use Social Media To Profit*

Testimonials

"A $112,500 Profit In 24 Hours!"

Hi Dan although it is not a penny stock, I found LNKD had earnings after hours on Feb 4, 2016. The historic chart of LNKD had some huge gaps during earnings. Feb 2, 2016 LNKD was trading at $200 per share so I bought the LNKD $150 Put option, 25 contracts for $.08 total cost per contract and the risk was just $200. Well in the after hours on Feb 4 LNKD fell to $93 and I almost sh*t my pants. I was $53 points in the money! Next morning I covered LNKD at $105 per share so I ended up being $45 in the money. 45 x 100 = $4500 x 25 contracts = $112,500 profit! It was my best trade ever. This never would have happened without your course and e-book. Thank you so much!

Mark - Sarasota, FL

"If You Liked Dan's First Courst Part Two Is Complete Gold"

After reading part one and watching the market move for many months, I was extremely excited to get part two and see the detailed trading plans and live screenshots. There are countless live trades explained in detail, and every single indicator and chart used is made completely clear both in the exact settings used and analysis of how every indicator works to analyze trading setups.

Part one and two, along with a couple months of experience, was enough to make me a consistently profitable day trader, something that typically takes years and many losses. Do yourself a favor, buy both parts of this series, and spend two months reading through and watching everything. Rather than giving your money away, invest in this material. You can easily make back the cost of this product with one trade after being armed with the knowledge inside. I know people who have spent thousands on gurus DVD's, videos, watch lists, etc (seriously thousands). I have a friend that let me watch his 8 hour DVD (supposedly the best trading DVD out there, that sells for $800). It was useful, but contained less than 20% of the valuable information found in the two parts of Dan's series. This literally leads you straight to a gold mine. If you are willing to put in the time to read and thoroughly learn the new info, I don't see how you couldn't profit!

Daniel - Fremont, CA

"You Definitetly WIll Make Money"

I was introduced to trading over 15 years ago. I studied different trading systems for microcaps and pennystocks and without a doubt Dan's system beats them all! Every other system will only tell you part of what you need to know in order to be successful. Dan tells you EVERYTHING. He takes you through the ABC's from which broker to use, all the way to money management and risk management. Everything is broken down so that even if you have absolutely NO prior knowledge of trading and are a complete novice, you will be able to understand and implement his system.

Emotion plays a huge part in undermining a trader however Dan's system is extremely MECHANICAL and virtually ELIMINATES the emotional aspect that hinders so many would-be traders. Dan's system doesn't just tell you the proper place to buy or sell...it consistently shows you how to calculate TO THE CENT when to buy or when to sell! No other system I have used, and I have used a lot, has every been able to do that. At least not with any kind of consistency and dependability.

Since using Dan's system I have become ridiculously confident in my trading, I have been able to keep out of trades that would've lost me money and I have taken trades that have done very well for me. I strongly suggest that anyone who is SERIOUS about making money in microcaps and penny stocks buy, buy, buy this course and read it at least four times and then apply it to the letter. You definitely will make money!

One final note...the support is absolutely superb. Whenever I had any questions Dan was extremely responsive and helpful through email and provided me with very detailed answers to my questions. Yet another truly pleasant surprise! Thanks so much Dan for releasing this valuable information!

Lawrence - Washington, DC

"Helped Me Immensely"

Dan your second book helped me immensely in not only my trading, but more simply my understanding of how the stock market works. I've tried other instructional products regarding trading stocks, but none have been more thorough and guided me as much as your second course and e-book. From the knowledge I have gained, I can now trade with confidence and know I have the necessary tools to be a successful trader. Thank so much!

Pat - Alhambra, CA

> ## "I Read Your Second Book And Wow!"
>
> Hey Dan I just wanted to say I read your second book and wow! You cover every-thing that a person should know to trade from the Blue Chips down to small caps. I honestly am I glad I paid for this. Thank you and good luck with your future trading!
>
> Nathan - Miami, FL

Guarantee

If you enjoyed my first book I am confident you are going to like my second even more. This book was designed for those people that really want to take trading serious and start extracting large profits from the stock market in the shortest period of time possible. It will help you to increase your confidence level so that you can become more comfortable with every trade that you make. With that said if you go through my second course and don't find it beneficial, I will be happy to provide a full refund during the first 60 days. Just contact me at support@beatstockpromoters.com.

http://www.beatstockpromoters.com/index2

Please note the order page opens in a new browser window. If it will not load it is probably due to your pop-up blocker. Please right click and then copy the URL and paste into your browser. Please read and agree to my disclaimer. By purchasing you agree that you have read and agree to the terms, conditions and the disclaimer.

Made in the USA
Middletown, DE
16 July 2019